C000000301

# LITTLE BOOK OF
# BRUNEL

Robin Jones

# LITTLE BOOK OF
# **BRUNEL**

First published in the UK in 2013

© Demand Media Limited 2013

www.demand-media.co.uk

Printed and bound in China

ISBN 978-1-909217-56-0

# Contents

# Brunel
## *Rediscover the legend*

Isambard Kingdom Brunel. Three names. Three people in one. Born in Portsmouth on 9 April 1806, there was Brunel the great engineer, who would habitually throw out the rulebook of tradition and established practice, and start again with a blank sheet of paper, taking the technology of the day to its limits – and then going another mile.

Then there was Brunel the visionary, who knew that transport technology had the power to change the world, and that he had the ability to deliver those changes.

Finally, there was Brunel the artist – who rarely saw technology as just functional, and strove to entwine the fruits of the Industrial Revolution with the elegance and grace of the neo-classical painter. His bridges, tunnels and railway infrastructure have entered a third century of regular use, and the beauty of their design and structure has rarely been equalled.

The three decades, from the 1830s to the 1850s, saw an explosion of technical excellence, and it was Brunel who in so many cases lit the blue touchpaper.

He did not always get it right first time, and it was left to others to reap the fruits of his many labours. Nevertheless, his actions fast-forwarded the march of progress by several decades.

In 2006, Britain is celebrating the 200th anniversary of  Brunel's birth, with a multitude of events large and small, for the family, the steam buff and the academic alike.

It will be a wonderful year, in which Isambard's many legacies will be re-examined – and revisited.

The landmarks will take centre stage, of course: the spectacular Royal Albert Bridge at Saltash, the magnificent glass-roofed terminus of Paddington, Maidenhead bridge with its elliptical arches that many said would never stand up, the stupendous Clifton Suspension Bridge, completed shortly after his death, to his design by a team of admirers, Bristol's original Temple Meads station, the Dawlish sea wall railway route – everyone's favourite section of the national network, and many more.

However, I hope that readers may use this commemorative volume as a travel guide to explore some of the lesser-known delights that he has bequeathed to us: the wonderful Bristol & Exeter Railway station at Bridgwater, the Wilts, Somerset & Weymouth Railway booking office at Bradford-on-Avon, and the lofty Devil's Bridge at Bleadon near Weston-super-Mare, to name but a few.

An excellent starting point is one of London's real hidden gems, the Brunel Engine House Museum at Rotherhithe, and its wonderful displays about the Thames Tunnel through which you can travel by underground train below.

Didcot Railway Centre in Oxfordshire is a must, with its demonstration and mixed-gauge running line and award-winning replica Fire Fly locomotive.

Don't miss out STEAM – Museum of the Great Western Railway in Swindon, which takes you on a unique journey through time to tell the story of God's Wonderful Railway and the man who created it, with North Star, the engine that made the line work, taking pride of place.

Then there's Bristol's Floating Harbour, one of the world's greatest waterfronts and, with many multi-million-pound development schemes in progress, getting better by the week. The jewel in its crown is, of course, the SS Great Britain, a vessel everyone should visit at least once in their life.

Brunel was the catalyst, which the Industrial Revolution needed to take it further to the next stage. He was by no means the only pioneer of his day, but perhaps more than anyone else, with the aid of the steam engine, provided the link between that great era of discovery and invention, and the modern world.

Why do we remain so fascinated by Brunel and his inventions? Maybe it is because he symbolises the swashbuckling hero we are all seeking in perpetuity, the person who really does have the power to bring the future to today.

*Robin Jones*

# Chapter 1

# Marc Brunel
## *The revolution begins*

What I find most amazing about Marc Isambard Brunel is that Hollywood has never seen fit to produce a blockbuster movie about him.

His story of world-shaping success has all the ingredients that you might expect from a late-18th century James Bond or Indiana Jones; a larger-than-life character who so often would throw caution to the wind, in the pursuit of a greater goal, regardless of the risks, with a classic fairytale romance thrown in.

Rejecting the life of a priest at an early age and cheating the guillotine, in Scarlet Pimpernel fashion, during the French Revolution – as would his future bride – Marc Brunel escaped to the United States, where made his name, before losing his fortune in England and winning it back again.

Not only that, but – most importantly – there would be a futuristic tunnel involved along the way – an essential ingredient in most Bond films. This one, however, would not be the fictional big-screen den of some sinister mastermind who wanted to take control of the world, but one which would genuinely change it in more ways than the young Marc could ever have imagined.

Furthermore, he would have a son who would not only follow in his engineering footsteps, but who, nearly two centuries after his birth, would take second place behind Sir Winston Churchill in a nationwide poll to find the greatest Briton of all time, even beating Shakespeare – not bad for someone who was half French.

Marc Brunel was born on 25 April 1769 in the hamlet of Hacqueville, near Rouen in France, the son of a wealthy farmer, Jean Charles Brunel, and his second wife, Marie Victoria Lefevre.

As soon as he could read and write, the young Marc displayed a talent for drawing, mathematics and mechanics.

His father, however, was having none of Marc's aspirations to become an engineer and join the new breed of pioneers spawned by the Industrial Revolution, on the other side of the English Channel.

Jean Charles insisted that his son had a career in the church, and so at the age of 11, he was sent to a seminary in Rouen.

There, the Superior saw that Marc's talents in drawing and woodwork would be better engaged elsewhere, especially as he had no religious leaning. So, it was arranged for him to stay with an elder cousin, Madam Carpentier, whose husband, a retired ship's captain, had become the American consul in Rouen.

While living with the Carpentiers, Marc attended the Royal College in Rouen, and excelled at mathematics, geometry, mechanics and drawing.

His scholarly success led him to a place as a cadet on the naval frigate Marechal de Castries and a six-year career at sea.

In January 1792, Marc returned home to find his native country embroiled in the worst excesses of the French Revolution. A Norman, and a staunch royalist sympathiser, he was at odds with the aims of the murderous Jacobins.

**LEFT** Samuel Drummond's portrait of Marc Brunel in later life, showing the Thames Tunnel, his greatest achievement.

ABOVE The fall of the Bastille on 14 July 1789. The ensuing Reign of Terror not only brought royalist Marc Brunel and his future wife together, but led to him fleeing France and making his fortune as an engineer in New York.

When, in January 1793, he made scathing remarks in a speech about the brutal Robespierre, during a visit to the Café de l'Echelle in Paris, he was lucky to escape a howling, revolutionary mob by the skin of his teeth, hiding in an inn for the night.

In Rouen, he found that the Carpentiers had a new guest, 17-year-old Sophia Kingdom.

She was the youngest of 16 children of Portsmouth naval-contractor, William Kingdom, who had died some years before. Her family had decided to send her to France with a friend, Monsieur de Longuemarre, and his English wife.

When a friend of the de Longuemarres was murdered by a mob for playing a royalist tune at a piano, the couple fled back to England, leaving Sophia behind, as she had been too ill to travel. At the Carpentiers' house, she fell in love with Marc Brunel.

Feeling the heat because of his sympathies with the Ancien Régime in France, and with Rouen in Jacobin hands, Marc fled the country for the USA, alone, but with the elaborate help of friends, amid justifiable fears for his safety.

He obtained a passport, after falsely claiming he was buying grain for the Navy, sailed away on the aptly named Liberty, and then established himself as a surveyor, architect and civil engineer in New York.

There, Marc built the old Bowery Theatre, in its day, the largest theatre in North America. He also built many other buildings, including an arsenal and a cannon foundry, as well as improving the defences between Staten and Long Island, and surveying a canal between Lake Champlain and the Hudson River at Albany.

He eventually took US citizenship and became chief engineer to the city of New York.

One of his designs won the competition for a new US capitol building to be built in Washington DC, but it was found too costly to implement and another plan was chosen instead.

While Marc prospered on the far side of the pond, Sophia remained in grave peril for her life.

Following the execution of Louis XVI and Marie Antoinette, Britain declared war on France, and all British nationals were imprisoned. Sophia found herself

in a convent at Gravelines, near Calais, which had been turned into a makeshift prison – complete with a guillotine. This, despite representations from the Carpentiers and Republican families, whose children she had taught English.

Sophia was not released until July 1794, when Robespierre was overthrown. The following year, she returned to her family's London home.

In February 1799, Marc decided to leave America and start again in England – perhaps driven by an all-consuming desire to renew his acquaintance with Sophia, whom he had never forgotten.

They were reunited in spring that year, and were married at the parish church of St Andrew in Holborn, on 1 November 1799, setting up their first

**ABOVE** The block mills in Portsmouth's dockyard where Marc Brunel set up shop on behalf of the Royal Navy, following his arrival from the USA.

**BELOW** Bust of Mark Brunel in the Brunel Engine House museum, above Thames Tunnel at Rotherhithe.

home in Bedford Street, Bloomsbury.

Marc had certainly not left his entrepreneurial spirit behind him in New York, in the first few weeks of his arrival in Britain; he had filed a patent for a 'duplicating, writing and

drawing machine'.

However, his big break came when the Government awarded him a £17,000 contract, after accepting his plans for mechanising the manufacture of pulley blocks for ships, which until then had been made by hand.

By 1808, a total of 43 machines of his design were installed in the naval dockyard at Portsmouth, where they became one of the earliest examples of all-mechanised production in the world.

With the machines, 10 men could do the job previously done by 100, and furthermore, Marc's blocks were superior in quality and consistency to the handmade predecessors.

The Brunels moved with their new daughter, Sophia, to a small terraced house in Portsea, near Portsmouth, from where Marc supervised the six-year project to build the block-making factory.

It was at this house in the early hours of 9 April 1806 that Isambard Kingdom Brunel was born.

Marc went on to design great, steam-powered machines for sawing and bending timber, some of which were also taken up by the Navy. He also

While the block-making operation was a success, the Navy proved to be slow at paying, and the Brunels needed a more regular income. Like everything that had gone before it, the sawmill was a success – Marc supplied the technology, Farthing the finance and business acumen.

All went well until Farthing retired in 1813, and then, without his hand on the tiller, the firm's finances fell into neglect.

The next year, the sawmills were all but destroyed in a fire, and Marc, when he finally looked at the bank balance, found the firm's finances to be far worse than he had thought.

Just to add to his financial woes, his army boot factory was dealt a major blow by Wellington's victory at Waterloo in 1815.

The Government decided to reduce the size of the Army, and Marc was left with a consignment of unwanted boots. He had to sell them off cheap to fund the rebuilding of the sawmills.

In the meantime, Marc, who had been elected to the Royal Society in 1814, had spent much time devising a series of new inventions, many of which were far less successful than his

**LEFT** The plaque, which marks the spot where Isambard Kingdom Brunel was born in Portsea.

worked on devices for stocking knitting and printing.

Horrified at the condition of the feet of soldiers returning from the Corunna campaign in 1809, Marc invented a series of machines to mass-produce boots and shoes, filing a patent the following year. His idea proved so successful that the Government asked him to expand production.

At Chatham's dockyard, Marc installed one of his sawmills, served by a rope-hauled railway with rails that were 7ft apart – much, much more of that later.

His success in the woodcutting field led to him joining forces in 1807, with a Mr Farthing, to set up a sawmill business in Battersea, and so Marc moved back to London with his family to oversee it.

# MARC BRUNEL - THE REVOLUTION BEGINS

ABOVE The modern-day replica of Richard Trevithick's 1804 steam railway locomotive, a world first, in action at the National Railway Museum's Railfest 2004 event in York, which marked the bicentenary of its first run. Marc Brunel and his son Isambard spent 10 years in vain trying to develop a gas-powered alternative. In the end Isambard would go for steam in a big way, but would still look for alternatives.

block-making equipment and saws.

In 1812, he experimented with steam navigation on the Thames, to no avail. He devised a series of compressed air engines, which turned out to be impracticable, designed a knitting machine, which nobody would buy, and entered into fruitless talks with the Russian Tsar, Alexander I, for a suspension bridge across the Neva River in St Petersburg.

Marc then came up with a handheld copying press, a device, which could make decorative packaging from tin foil and also began work on a rotary press for the Times newspaper.

Disaster hit in 1820, when, after years

of continual, habitual neglect of the financial, rather than, technological side of his ailing business empire, his bankers, Sykes & Co, were now insolvent, and nobody would honour his cheques.

Marc and Sophia could no longer pay their debts and on 14 May 1821, were hauled off to the King's Bench debtors' prison, where they spent three months – until influential friends, led by the Duke of Wellington, managed to persuade the Government to stump up £5000, lest the inventor's services be lost to Russia, where the Tsar had shown renewed interest in his Neva River scheme.

Able to pay off his crippling debts at last, Marc resumed his career in a far more humble manner, becoming a consulting engineer in an office at 29 Poultry, in the City of London.

Young Isambard Kingdom Brunel had, in the meantime, been groomed by his father to take over the business.

Marc taught his son drawing and geometry, before sending him to Dr Morell's boarding school in Hove.

While at the school, Isambard carried out a survey of the town and made many drawings of the houses there.

At the age of 14, he was sent to France to finish his schooling at the College of Caen, in Normandy, and progressed from there, to the Lycée Henri-Quatre in Paris. He also studied at the Institution de M Massin.

His father had also arranged for him to have an apprenticeship under Louis Breguet, the world-famous maker of clocks, chronometers and other scientific instruments.

While his father underwent what the family described as his 'misfortune', Isambard had been abroad, not returning to England until August 1822, at the age of 16.

He immediately took up work in his father's office, working alongside him on designs for a cannon-boring mill for the Netherlands government, the rotary printing press – amongst much else, including two suspension bridges for the French Government for the Île de Bourbon (Reunion) off Mauritius.

The father-and-son team worked on more mechanical engineering designs, and came up with the first double-acting marine engine, which set on

course a chain of events, which would lead Isambard to worldwide fame and glory.

Two years before Isambard had been born, in 1804, a Cornish mining engineer named Richard Trevithick had sown the seeds of a transport revolution which would change the face of, and shrink, the globe: the first railway locomotive.

While Ironbridge is widely regarded today as the cradle of the Industrial

**LEFT** The bust of Isambard Kingdom Brunel in Rotherhithe's excellent museum in the Brunel Engine House.

Revolution, necessity was very much the mother of invention in the wilds of Cornwall, where the landscape so beloved by holidaymakers today, resembled the Black Country or South Wales coalfields in their heyday, being littered with the engine houses, processing mills and slag heaps of various tin, copper, lead and arsenic mines.

The biggest problem for mining was keeping the tunnels free of water, and some of those in Cornwall stretched out beneath the sea. It was the stationary steam engine, which provided a satisfactory means of pumping out water so that the mines could be worked safely.

All well and good, but there was the difficulty in transporting large, steam-engine components from manufacturers like Boulton & Watt of Birmingham, to the Duchy for assembly - Cornwall was never connected to the canal network, which had made the Industrial Revolution 'happen' and its mining areas lay in hilly terrain that were mainly accessed only by sea.

But, what if a machine could move by itself to the site where it was to work, instead of being dragged there by horses?

Furthermore, what if it could pull

other machines, and maybe even carry people?

Trevithick, who was born on 13 April 1771, did not invent the first machine that could move itself using the power of steam.

That honour goes to Austro-Hungarian army officer Nicholas Joseph Cugnot, who wanted to devise a more efficient means of moving heavy artillery than horses, resulting in the world's first steam tractor, which appeared in 1769, with a refined prototype displayed in Paris the following year.

Cugnot's invention was a clumsy and overweight device, with appalling steering, or lack of it, and which could operate for only 20 minutes before it needed to cool down and have fresh water added – not exactly an asset in battle. His work came to an abrupt end when his weighty machine overturned in a busy street.

Meanwhile in Britain, Scotsman William Murdoch had been experimenting with steam traction while working for Boulton & Watt as its Cornish agent, and in 1784, his first working model hauled a wagon around a room, inside his Redruth home.

Murdoch then gave an infamous outdoor trial to a 19in-long, three-wheeled steam carriage one night along the narrow lane leading to the town's church. The machine ran off without him, at 8mph, and terrified the rector, who believed that the devil was about to attack him.

Undeterred, Murdoch built an improved model and apparently a further two carriages as well – and they were seen not only by the townsfolk of Redruth but, also by the young Richard Trevithick.

However, Murdoch's work ceased towards the end of the 1790s, and he is better remembered as the man who invented gaslight, using it to light his Redruth home.

Trevithick, however, was working on increasing steam pressure, so that he could make smaller engines. He quickly realised that if a much-smaller engine could power a machine or pump, then it could also be capable of being adapted to drive itself.

Forming a partnership with Andrew Vivian, he launched his own steam carriage on Christmas Eve 1801, when it successfully climbed Camborne Hill under its own power.

Several onlookers ecstatically jumped

**LEFT** Isambard Kingdom Brunel, as painted by his brother-in-law JC Horsley, in 1833.

aboard and rode on it – making it the world's first motorcar.

There was jubilation all round and those involved in the escapade celebrated at the inn at the top – leaving the locomotive to burn out.

Two subsequent experiments with steam carriages in London proved unsuccessful, purely because of the unsurfaced roads of the day, so Trevithick sought a medium, which could support their great weight – the railway.

In 1802, he began work on building a railway locomotive for use at Coalbrookdale ironworks in Shropshire, near the site of the world's first iron bridge, although it was not believed to have run in public. He was then asked to install a high-pressure locomotive to run from Penydarren ironworks near Merthyr Tydfil, along the horse-drawn tram road that linked the works to the Glamorganshire Canal at Abercynon wharf, and jumped at the opportunity.

On February 21 1804, Trevithick's engine hauled a rake of loaded wagons, plus 70 men, along the full length of the tramway, immediately earning him the accolade of the world's first railway locomotive engineer. However, the cast-iron plates, which formed the rails, cracked under the weight of the engine in several places.

Trevithick then built a similar locomotive at Gateshead for use on the Wylam Colliery waggonway in 1805, but the mine owners decided not to buy it, probably because their railway's rails were made of wood, so, it was converted to blow the furnace, as a stationary engine.

In 1808, Trevithick turned out his last steam railway locomotive, Catch-Me-Who-Can, which ran on a circle of track in fairground fashion for public gaze - ironically very near to the site of the future Euston station. With its carriage, it became the world's first, steam passenger train.

Trevithick made little money from his railway experiments, and turned away from steam traction for the last time, sadly accepting that the horse and cart, whether on rails, roads or a canal towpath, still reigned supreme.

It was unlikely that Trevithick ever envisaged a national network of railways; he merely intended his engines to replace horses on the short tramways, which served canals, harbours and other transhipment points for industrial products or supplies.

Not everyone was as pessimistic. In 1812, the need for a serious alternative to horses arose out of the relentless demands for their supply and use in the continuing war between Britain and Napoleon.

England's north-east, like Cornwall, had no connection to the national waterway network, so, another form of bulk transport was needed, and fast.

Christopher Blackett, who owned Wylam Colliery, failed to persuade Trevithick to have one last attempt at railway engines. Meanwhile William Hedley and Timothy Hackworth obliged, and with the aid of engine-wright Jonathan Forster, built the legendary eight-wheeled, eight-ton Puffing Billy for the mine's tramway system, drawing much inspiration from Trevithick's designs.

George Stephenson, who was later to become a close friend of Isambard Brunel, built his first engine in 1815, and the world's first steam-powered public line, the Stockton and Darlington Railway, which Stephenson helped engineer, opened in 1825.

Among Brunel's circle of friends was another Cornishman, Sir Humphrey Davy, a chemist who discovered the anaesthetic effect of nitrous oxide (laughing gas) and invented a safety lamp for use in coal mines, allowing deep seams to be mined, despite the presence of methane. Considered to be Britain's leading scientist, in 1812 he was knighted by George III.

Davy and his assistant, Michael Faraday, found that several gases could be liquefied by a combination of low temperature and very high pressure, and in 1823 Marc Brunel became convinced that their discoveries could form the basis of a more efficient type of engine to rival the steam variety.

For much of the ensuing decade, Marc and Isambard spent their time experimenting with pressurised carbonic gas, in a bid to break new ground in a fertile age for new inventions, to produce what they called the Gaz Engine, but despite throwing £15,000 of the father's money at the project, it could not be made to work. This would be a rare example of a Brunel failure, despite their perseverance.

Railways would have to wait, however, for in 1823, Marc Brunel began work on what would be his greatest project of all – the Thames Tunnel.

# Chapter 2

# The Thames Tunnel
## *The eighth wonder of the world*

We Britons are by and large a modest bunch, maybe too modest for our own good. For instance, had it been a US citizen who had invented the world's first steam locomotive, and not Richard Trevithick, we would never hear the last of it.

Our nation oozes heritage out of every orifice, yet so much of it we have passed by, or let disappear without trace, before we realise its importance.

In a back street in London's Rotherhithe stands a small, yellow-stone industrial building, which stands out only because it has a tall chimney and unlike the surrounding properties, is not a domestic dwelling.

Those intent on visiting the capital to see the Tower of London, Buckingham Palace or St Paul's Cathedral would not give it a second glance, and in any case, Rotherhithe is well off the beaten tourist track.

Yet, in so many ways, this structure is far more important than any of the aforementioned, at least in terms of the development of the modern world.

Now known as the Brunel Museum (formerly the Brunel Engine House), this humble building in Railway Avenue should be a first port of call, for it is a veritable mine of discovery – if only for the fact that it was built to drain the world's first public, underwater tunnel.

Today tunnels beneath the Thames are commonplace, and building one

would hardly grab the headlines. We have tunnels for underground trains, road traffic, essential services like gas, water and electricity, telecommunications and even a secret network of corridors between government buildings, it is believed.

However, back in the 19th century, when Britain led the world in technology, the Thames Tunnel was hailed as its eighth wonder, and with much justification.

To gauge its importance, we have to imagine ourselves back in the London of 200 years ago, when the sole means of crossing the river was by way of the medieval London Bridge, or by using ferrymen.

The first enclosed docks opened in 1802 on the Isle of Dogs, and within 20 years it had been followed by the East India Docks at Blackwall, London Docks at Wapping, and Surrey Docks at Rotherhithe. Downstream from the Tower of London, both sides of the river were crammed with warehouses and factories, but the river placed a major stumbling block to lines of communication and trade.

The volume of traffic on the water caused much congestion, and it was obvious that a new physical crossing would be needed. However, a bridge would have to be high enough to clear the masts of ships, and the technology for a lifting structure on the lines of the later Tower Bridge had not yet been developed.

Thoughts turned towards the building of a tunnel, but no blueprint for the construction of one was readily available.

It was said that in the ancient world, the Assyrian queen Semiramis had the River Euphrates at Babylon diverted, so a tunnel could be built beneath it, for her personal use, and some believed that the Romans bored beneath the sea off Marseille.

In recent times, tunnels under the sea for mining purposes, off the west coast of Cornwall and beneath the estuary of the River Tyne had been hacked through rock, but these were not built

for public use and did not have to contend with the soft ground normally found under riverbeds. Master that single problem – and a Thames tunnel could be built.

In 1798, Ralph Dodd, the designer of the Grand Surrey Canal, proposed a 900-yard tunnel between Gravesend and Tilbury and obtained sufficient money to sink a shaft, but was not able to raise further funds after geological problems were encountered.

Four years later, Robert Vazie drew up plans for a shorter tunnel on the narrower part of the river between Rotherhithe and Limehouse, and joined forces with none other than fellow Cornish mining expert, Richard

**BELOW** The River Thames above the Thames Tunnel.

Trevithick, to build it under the auspices of the Thames Archway Company, which was duly founded in 1805.

Work on digging a 5ft-high pilot tunnel at a depth of 76ft feet began at Rotherhithe in August 1807 and progressed at the rate of 6ft per day, speeding up when Trevithick took sole charge.

After the tunnel crossed the halfway point, a layer of rock was encountered, beyond which lay quicksand – which in turn brought water flooding into the tunnel, causing part of the roof to collapse.

Undeterred, the miners pressed on, draining the tunnel after blocking the hole. There were more inrushes of water, however, including one, which nearly drowned Trevithick on 26 January 1808, after the low-tide mark on the north bank of the Thames had been reached.

Trevithick, who left only when the water was up to his neck, repaired the breach by dumping clay onto the riverbed before pumping the tunnel dry.

To counteract such problems, he devised a new method by which the tunnel would be built from above. The miners would work inside a series of cofferdams and lay a tunnel, comprising of cast-iron sections inside their trench.

However, it had never been done before, and his company's directors and financial backers were having none of it, instead offering a prize of £500 to anyone who could find another means of finishing the tunnel. When none of the 49 offered solutions were deemed workable, the tunnel was abandoned, with less than 200ft to go.

In 1818, however, Marc Brunel patented a tunnelling shield; a device that made it possible to safely bore through water-bearing strata such as the offending quicksand.

While Marc had been engaged with his sawmill at Chatham Dockyard, he studied the destructive shipworm, teredo navalis, which ate its way through timber with its hard, horny head, leaving a coating around the 'tunnel' it had gnawed.

He had already looked at the possibility of a tunnel under the River Neva for the Russian Tsar, and in doing so had brought himself up to speed with the technical problems that would be involved.

His revolutionary shield consisted of 12 separate numbered cast-iron frames,

**BELOW** As the tunnel is an International Landmark Site, when it was refurbished in the 1990s, four of the original arches were preserved as built.

comprising a total of 36 cells in which a miner could work independently of the others.

The propulsion for the device was provided by a screw, which drove the shield forward in 4.5-inch steps, the width of a brick.

The frames with the odd numbers were worked first, and as each board was replaced, it was braced with polling screws against the adjacent cell. When all the boards had been worked down, the shield could move forward and the screws were replaced. The main frame would be worked forward by the use of screw jacks bracing against brickwork behind. Each foot of tunnel required 5500 bricks to be laid.

Brunel's 1818 patent had detailed a circular boring shield, with long rotary cutting blades at the front to excavate the earth, and a cylinder supporting the top and sides, until a brick lining could be built.

However, during his time in the debtor's prison, he realised that it could not be implemented with the steam-engine technology available at the time, and so opted for a rectangular shield instead, with all the digging done by hand, in the time-honoured way.

Marc's old ally the Duke of Wellington lent his support for a fresh scheme to burrow beneath the river, and the Thames Tunnel Company was formed in 1824, with Brunel as engineer.

A shaft was sunk at Rotherhithe on 2 March 1825, using a groundbreaking method of building its 42ft-high, 900-ton brick cylinder at ground level and then allowing it to sink under its weight down the hole excavated below.

By July, the shaft had been sunk to a depth of 65ft, allowing the assembly of the shield to take place.

By November, tunnelling towards the Thames had begun, with Marc optimistic that the project would be finished within three years.

Isambard was appointed acting resident engineer on April 1826, and given

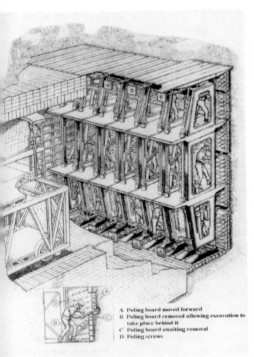

A Poling board moved forward
B Poling board removed allowing excavation to take place behind it
C Poling board awaiting removal
D Poling screws

make a quick buck, capitalised on the publicity that the project was generating, by allowing paying sightseers inside the first 300ft of the tunnel from February 1827.

The project, however, would not progress as efficiently as Marc predicted. The first of five major floods took place on 18 May 1827, caused by tunnelling too close to the riverbed. Visiting the bottom of the river in a diving bell, as crowds watched from the riverbank, Isambard realised that gravel dredgers had caused the problem.

A 10,000sq ft canvas sheet was ordered by Marc to be placed over the breach, weighed down with chains around its edges, so that 4000 bags of clay could be laid on it to fill the depression, before the floodwaters could be pumped out.

the job permanently, when he was just 20, on 3 January the following year.

He would stay below ground for 36 hours at a time to supervise the tunnelling, and became ill in the process.

The company directors, eager to

Regardless of the danger, tourists were taken inside the tunnel by punt to inspect the damage as it was being repaired. One miner was drowned when the punt overturned in the flooded

workings, becoming the second fatality on the project, the first being when a drunken workman had fallen down a shaft.

The tunnel was cleared of water by November, and Marc was so pleased that he organised a banquet in the tunnel to celebrate. Up to 50 guests sat around a linen-covered table as the tunnel was illuminated by four massive candelabras, as the band of the Coldstream Guards provided musical entertainment. Around 120 miners and bricklayers also attended, and Isambard (Marc was not present) was presented with a pickaxe and shovel.

The miners faced an extremely hazardous and unpleasant task, despite the use of the innovative shield, while assistant engineer Richard Beamish had lost an eye during the work.

Not only was ventilation difficult, and there was the threat of drowning if breaches occurred, but there was the ever-present danger of both poisonous gases and cholera from the foul Thames water. The river at this time was little better than an open sewer, as it was to be many years before Joseph Bazalgette implemented his effluent drainage system for the capital. A fever that caused blindness was rife among the workers and in November 1825, Marc also fell ill.

His son also narrowly escaped death when water burst into the tunnel again, on 12 January 1828. Having managed to free a timber beam, which trapped his leg, Isambard found that the workmen's stairs were blocked by miners panicking to escape - so he turned and headed for the separate visitors' stairs instead.

A huge wave of water swept through the tunnel, swamping Isambard – but also carrying him to safety at the top of the 42ft Rotherhithe shaft. However, six workmen, including two who had been working with Isambard when the inundation occurred, died.

The flood led the directors to abandon the tunnel, which by then had reached 605ft. Not good news at a time when the country was suffering from an economic slump; the tunnel had

drained all the available finances, after 30 times the amount of clay used to repair the first breach had been dumped on the riverbed to allow the workings to be pumped dry again.

Wellington again offered his support; publicly appealing for £200,000 to be subscribed to finish the job, but only £9,600 was raised.

So, in August that year, the tunnel face and shield were bricked up, but the sightseers were still allowed a glimpse inside the workings, by means of a mirror. The Times dismissed the project as the 'Great Bore'.

Meanwhile, Isambard's injuries had been far worse than he first thought, and he spent several months convalescing in Brighton, during which time he suffered the first of a series of haemorrhages.

Marc continued to rally support for the tunnel and designed a better shield. He suffered a heart attack in November 1831, but carried on regardless, so determined were he and his son to finish the project.

At last, in December 1835, Wellington and another of Marc's friends in high places, Lord Althorp, approved a loan of £270,000 – and boring restarted on 24 March 1835 – by which time

ABOVE A Yates' watercolour sketch of the top of the Thames Tunnel shaft at Rotherhithe and the engine house next to it, built by Marc Brunel in 1842 and now a scheduled ancient monument.

Isambard had become heavily involved elsewhere, on steamship and railway projects.

There were further major breaches of the riverbed on 23 August 1837, 3 November 1837, when a worker sleeping in the shield was drowned, and on 20 March 1838.

On 22 August 1839, the tunnel reached the low-water mark on the Wapping side, and in June the following year, work on sinking a shaft on the north bank began.

For his work on the project, Marc Brunel was knighted by Queen Victoria, on 24 March 1841. However, at the age of 72, the tunnel work had already taken its toll on his health.

Finally, on 16 November 1841, engineer Thomas Page ran excitedly to Marc's house with the news that the tunnel had at last reached the shaft

on the north shore.

Finances had been drained to the extent that the proposed spiral road ramps to take traffic into the tunnel could no longer be afforded. Instead, as a result, it would only be accessible to pedestrians by means of winding staircases at either end.

It was like spending your life savings on building a Rolls-Royce, to then only be able to fit a seat for the driver. Without the carriageways and the ability to claim tolls from road traffic, the tunnel would never be profitable.

Sightseers were allowed into the northern shaft for the first time in August 1842, and after Marc suffered a stroke on 7 November, Isambard took over many of his dealings with the company's directors regarding engineering matters.

The completed two-bore tunnel - which has a roof only 14ft below the riverbed and is 1200ft long between both shafts – was finally opened amid much fanfare on 25 March 1843.

Thames watermen flew black flags from their vessels because they knew that their trade was now at an end.

However, others had paid a much higher price. While the official death toll among workers was only seven, it had been suggested that the 'real' death toll was likely to have exceeded 20 and may even have been closer to 200, taking into account the consequences of work-related illnesses, and illness caused by working in the stifling atmosphere.

Queen Victoria gave the tunnel her seal of approval when, with little warning, she turned up at Wapping by royal barge on 26 July 1843, with her consort Prince Albert, and accompanied by Page (who was standing in for Marc Brunel who was away on business) and company directors, walked the full length of the tunnel from Wapping to Rotherhithe and back.

About 50,000 people walked through the tunnel during the first two days of operation, and more than a million people used it in the first four months. People travelled from far and wide to see what was heralded as a great marvel, and a roaring trade in souvenirs - trin-

ket boxes, whisky flasks and jugs, and paper peep-show models, a distant forerunner of today's hugely popular red, pottery telephone boxes, black cabs and model buses - quickly sprang up.

However, it had its critics, not least of all those who found the 99 steps at each end too much to bear - and who preferred the old ferries. The American novelist, Nathaniel Hawthorne, was less than impressed by his visit and wrote in 1855:

"It consisted of an arched corridor of apparently interminable length, gloomily lighted with jets of gas at regular intervals... there are people who spend their lives there, seldom or never, I presume, seeing any daylight, except perhaps a little in the morning.

"All along the extent of this corridor, in little alcoves, there are stalls of shops, kept principally by women, who, as you approach, are seen through the dusk

RIGHT Two early souvenirs celebrating the Thames Tunnel: a lacquered box and a hip flask.

offering for sale multifarious trumpery. So far as any present use is concerned, the tunnel is an entire failure."

Sadly, the tunnel quickly became the den of prostitutes, pickpockets and ne'er-do-wells in need of a free place to sleep at night. Furthermore, it did not solve the traffic problem of London, as trade and population continued to soar, and it was soon clear that more river crossings would be needed.

After the tunnel was finished, Marc and his wife moved from Rotherhithe to Park Street, a short walk away from Isambard's house in Duke Street.

Marc died on 12 December 1849, and was buried in Kensal Green Cemetery. Sophia moved in with her son, and lived until January 1855.

Three years before his death, Marc was said to have approved of his tunnel being converted for use as a railway. In 1865, it was sold to the East London Railway for £200,000 and tracks were laid through it so that it could carry steam trains between Wapping & Shadwell station and New Cross. The first services ran on 7 December 1869.

The tunnel eventually became part of the electrified underground system, and is still in daily service today.

In 1869, work on building a second tunnel beneath the Thames began – the 1235ft Tower Subway, a 7ft-diameter, iron tube which runs 18ft below the riverbed between Great Tower Hill on the north side of the river, and Tooley Street on the south.

A smaller affair than Brunel's original, it was designed to convey a narrow gauge, cable-hauled railway and opened on 12 April 1870. The single carriage was insufficient to carry the volume of passengers wanting to cross the river, and so the line was closed on 7 December that year with the tunnel converted into a pedestrian subway, reached by 96 steps. Nonetheless, the Tower Subway has staked its claim to being the first purpose-built tube railway tunnel.

It was, however, predated by the Thames Tunnel by 20 years, and it was the Brunels who proved to London that crossing the Thames underneath the river was possible.

Their innovation, improved by the methods used by James Henry Greathead and his cylindrical boring

**THAMES TUNNEL.**

THE ANNUAL

**FANCY FAIR,**

WILL TAKE PLACE ON

**MONDAY, MARCH 22, 1852,**

*and continue all the Week.*

The Amusements in this wonderful Work of Art, will be unusually attractive. The illuminations by Gas and Variegated Lamps will be on a very extensive scale.

Boggett's patent Prismatic Reflectors, Have been added to the Leslie Gas Burners, increasing the light upwards of twenty per cent.

**GRAND MOVING PANORAMA**

Painted on upwards of 20,000 feet of canvass, comprising views of the Thames and London, from Westminster to Blackwall.

**COSMORAMIC VIEWS, MUSIC BY STEAM,**

THE BEAUTIFUL

*Metal Model of the Shield*

Invented by the late Sir I. Brunel, and used by him with the greatest security in the construction of the Thames Tunnel, is now added to this collection.

**ELECTRICITY,**

**FANCY GLASS BLOWING,**

Patent Weighing, Lifting, & Striking Machines.

**A Ball Room 150 Feet long.**

**THE MYSTERIOUS LADY,**

CATLIN'S NEW PAVILION OF ARTS,

Where a correct LIKENESS can be taken in TWO MINUTES

**THE GREAT AMERICAN WIZARD,**

*Indian and Chinese Exhibition, The Montreal Minstrels,*

MR. E. GREEN, the celebrated Bottle

**PANTOMIMIC EQUILIBRIST.**

**MR. W. PERRY'S** celebrated BRASS BAND in Uniform, will attend.

New and Commodious Rooms for Refreshments, and Stalls for the sale of every kind of Fancy Articles. In addition to the above attractions, the much admired FRESCO PAINTINGS, 32 in number, by I. B. Henkon, which are now quite complete, will be open to the public without any extra charge beyond the usual Toll of ONE PENNY.

*The Tunnel is perfectly dry; the roads requiring to be watered each day to prevent dust.*

**TOLL as usual ONE PENNY. OPEN DAY & NIGHT**

E. Batt, Printer, Rotherhithe.

**LEFT** A handbill advertising a fair in the Thames Tunnel.

shield (more akin to the circular shield in Brunel's 1818 patent than the rectangular one used for the Thames Tunnel) in building the Tower Subway, laid firm foundations for the London underground railway network, without which London would quickly grind to a standstill.

In turn, the availability of safe, soft-ground tunnelling technology inspired cities throughout the world to build their own underground systems, and even the construction of the Channel Tunnel has roots in Marc Brunel's original shield design.

Many accolades therefore must go to Marc Brunel, his son and the Thames Tunnel. However, the Brunels could – and should – have been beaten by Trevithick a third of a century earlier.

The Cornishman's plan to complete his tunnel by laying cast-iron pipe sections behind cofferdams may not have won the support of his company, but has since been shown to work, and in recent times has been employed in the building of the San Francisco BART (Bay Area Rapid Transit) tunnel and the Detroit river tunnel, for instance.

In later life, after abandoning his railway locomotive ventures, Trevithick

**FAR LEFT** The famous banquet held inside the incomplete tunnel in 1827.

**LEFT** A contemporary sketch of floodwaters breaking through into the tunnel workings.

sought his fortune in the mines of South America, along with many of his fellow Cornishmen. He did not find it, returned home in poverty, died in Dartford on 22 April 1833, and was buried at a now-unmarked grave in the town's churchyard.

A year later, the Bodmin & Wade- bridge Railway became Cornwall's first steam-hauled line. In the decade that followed, a young engineer was to make mind-blowing advances in the field of railways, linking Trevithick's home county to the capital in the process. His name was Isambard Kingdom Brunel.

# Chapter 3

# Reach For The Sky
## *Bristol and its suspension bridge*

"Exertions with actresses!" Isambard Brunel's biographers gave that reason as to why he suffered a major relapse during his convalescence in Brighton, where he had gone to recover from the extensive injuries sustained during the aforementioned collapse of the Thames Tunnel.

Whatever the reason, he was despatched first of all to a relative's house in Plymouth and then on to the genteel Bristol area of Clifton, in a bid to accelerate his recuperation. History would never look back.

Once there, Isambard, still just 22, found he was equally as inspired by the sight of the limestone Avon Gorge, as he had been by the ladies of Brighton.

For him, it was a classic case of being in the right place at the right time.

In 1753, William Vick, a local alderman, left £1000 to be invested until such time as it had grown into £10,000 – when it was to be spent on a bridge spanning the gorge.

By 1829, the figure of £8000 had been reached, and a committee was set up not only to raise the remaining £2000 but to hold a competition to find the best design, with a prize of 100 guineas for the winner. And Isambard was right on the doorstep.

He eagerly presented the Clifton Bridge Committee with a choice of four designs, all involving a suspension bridge, with spans varying from 870ft to

916ft – with more than a little help from father Marc regarding the finer detail.

The great canal and bridge builder, Thomas Telford, was called in to judge the contest, which attracted 22 entries.

However, Telford dismissed them all, including Isambard's design, saying that his proposed span was too long – citing his own troubles with lateral movement caused by wind on his own Menai Strait suspension bridge, which was less than 600ft wide.

The committee then asked Telford to draw up a scheme of his own, and he produced plans for a suspension bridge, supported by two ornate Gothic towers set into the bed of the gorge.

A furious Isambard poured scorn on

**ABOVE** Clifton Suspension Bridge – still magnificent more than 140 years after it was completed.

**LEFT** The celebrations at the opening of Clifton Suspension Bridge on 8 December 1864.

the Telford design in a scathing letter to the bridge committee, and then, his finances dwindling, set off to the north of England to look for work.

He was turned down for the post of engineer to the Newcastle & Carlisle Railway in favour of Francis Giles, who at one time had tried to replace Marc Brunel as engineer of the Thames Tunnel.

However, his disappointment was assuaged somewhat when, on 10 June 1830, he was elected a Fellow of the Royal Society, in recognition of his work on the tunnel, his plans for the Clifton bridge and his experiments with the Gaz Engine. He also found a rather unglamorous job to earn some desperately needed income – draining marshland at Tollesbury, in Essex.

Suddenly, on 16 March 1831, the bridge committee announced that Isambard's scheme had won a second contest, although to allay fears aroused by the apparently jealous Telford, its members agreed to (unnecessarily) spend an extra £14,000, to add a stone abutment rising out of the rocks at Leigh Woods, to shorten the overall span to 630ft.

Apart from this modification, Isambard was given a free hand to design the final product, and he came up with a blueprint for a 240ft-high, chain support towers, and an elaborate cast-iron ornamentation on the pillars. He called the project his 'Egyptian thing' because of its style, and it was to have sphinxes on top of each pillar, as per the pyramids.

Isambard attended the launch ceremony for the

**BELOW** Crowds flock to the opening of Clifton Suspension Bridge.

**ABOVE** A hand-coloured, early-20th century postcard adds impact to Brunel's design.

suspension bridge on 21 June 1831 – only to be told shortly afterwards by the committee that they did not yet have enough funds to build it.

That year, he was caught up in Reform Bill riots in Bristol. The Bill aimed to widen the electorate, so that Members of Parliament would be seen to be elected, not just by a handful of powerful landowners but, by the public at large.

On 29 October, a stone-throwing mob stormed the Mansion House, official residence of the city mayor, in Queen's Square, after the Conservative recorder of Bristol, Sir Charles Wetherell, who opposed the Bill, arrived for the assizes, along with a detachment of dragoon guards under Lt Col Brereton, who went on to side with the mob rather than charge against it.

The following day, Isambard and a

**BELOW** Isambard Brunel designed this wrought iron, tubular, swing bridge to span the entrance to his South Lock, on Bristol's Floating Harbour. Superseded in the 1960s by the electrically operated Plimsoll Bridge, which carries the A38 above the river, with the old bridge preserved beneath it. Brunel was a pioneer of tubular bridge construction, as evident in the later Royal Albert Bridge at Saltash.

friend, Nicholas Roch, were sworn in as special constables, after Brereton took his troops out of the city, and the Mansion House, Bishop's Palace and toll houses were all looted and burned by the crowd. Isambard caught a looter, but he escaped.

A fortnight later, ever searching for an income, Isambard went to Wearside, where local merchants and business-men gave him the job of designing a dock for Monkwearmouth.

His plans for what would become North Dock were at first rejected by Parliament, but the scheme went ahead in 1838, under the able supervision

of Thames Tunnel bricklayer, Michael Lane.

However, the site chosen by Isambard's clients proved difficult for navigation and the dock was little used. In recent times it has become a pleasure boat marina.

Returning south, Isambard visited the Stockton & Darlington Railway, which had become the first steam-hauled public railway in the world, when it opened in 1825. He had his first trip on a steam train on 5 December 1831 on the Liverpool & Manchester Railway, the world's first inter-city line, which had opened the year before.

Despite the nationwide public-ity, which had been afforded to the Liverpool & Manchester, Isambard was not easily impressed, and his mind began working overtime with regard to the improvements he wanted to make to it. In his diary he wrote: "I record this specimen of the shaking on Manchester railway. The time is not far off when we shall be able to take our coffee and write, while going noiselessly and smoothly at 45mph – let me try."

When the Reform Act was passed in 1832 and riots ended, confidence returned to both the country and

Bristol. Money was made available for the improvement of the city's Floating Harbour, which had been created by canal engineer, William Jessop, between 1804-10, by damming the River Avon, at Cumberland Basin and near Temple Meads, and diverting the Avon through a new channel to the south of the city centre.

Before, ships would be left high and dry in the city harbour because of the 30ft difference between high and low tide, Jessop's pioneering scheme allowed ships to stay afloat, without risk of grounding on the muddy bottom of the river estuary.

The Floating Harbour had brought prosperity to the city, and the Committee for Bristol Docks – of which Roch was a member – sought further improvements to the artificial navigation.

In 1832, Roch brought in Isambard, who advised on the installation of sluices and an underfall dam at Rownham, for regulating water inflow and scouring silt.

In 1843, Isambard also came up with a steam-powered drag boat, Bertha, to move silt from the dock walls and she remained in service until 1968.

He also designed a new, south-entrance lock, completed in 1849, which used the first-ever wrought-iron buoyant gate.

Isambard's work in Bristol greatly raised his standing in the port, and as we shall see, opened the door for arguably some of his greatest triumphs.

Eventually, more funds were raised for the Clifton bridge project, and the

**BELOW** The Clifton Suspension Bridge is a rare example of an instance where a man-made structure has enhanced its natural setting.

Marquess of Northampton, president of the British Association for the Advancement of Science, laid the foundation stone on 27 August 1836.

As work began, a one-and-a-half-inch thick, 1000ft-long iron bar was laid across the gorge to allow both materials and men to be moved from one pier to the other. On the first occasion it was

**ABOVE** Brunel's South Lock was taken out of use in 1879 when a larger one was built to the north. Incidentally, the B Bond warehouse in the distance is now home to the Create Centre, an interactive attraction based on environmental excellence and run by the city council.

being manoeuvred into position, the capstan used to wind it over the great gap failed, and the bar plunged into the river below, becoming entangled with a passing ship.

To everyone's surprise, Isambard insisted that despite this calamity, he would ride in the next basket to cross the wire from one bank to another. Everyone watching was mortified when the basket became stuck in the middle of the bar.

With certain death awaiting in the yawning chasm below, Isambard swung himself up from the basket to the bar and freed it.

Was his act of derring-do, sheer courage, or the best form of self-advertisement that he could ever have wished for?

Nonetheless, locals paid to be hauled across the gap by the bar when work was not in progress.

However, financial problems continued to haunt the scheme, with the main contractor going bankrupt in 1837, leaving the bridge trustees to run the project by themselves.

It seemed in 1843 that the bridge was all but complete, but a glance at the accounts revealed that on top of the £45,000 spent to date, an extra £30,000 was needed.

After another decade of struggling to pay off debts, the trustees were left in 1853 with no option but to sell off the fixtures and fittings, leaving the unfinished piers on either side of the gorge.

The chains went to another Brunel project, the Royal Albert Bridge at Saltash, but more of that later.

An offer in 1857 to finish the Clifton project on the cheap, by using ropes instead of chains, was met with scorn by Isambard, and there was serious talk of demolishing the piers and abandoning the scheme altogether.

Isambard would never see his magnificent bridge finished, but a year after his death in 1859, the Institute of Civil Engineers decided to complete the bridge as a monument to the man who by then had become acclaimed as one of the greatest engineers of all time.

After receiving parliamentary approval in 1861, and with £35,000 capital, a new company was formed, appointing renowned engineers William Barlow and John Hawkshaw to do the job, but on a simpler scale than that envisaged by Isambard.

Isambard had designed a suspension footbridge, the Hungerford Bridge, in London in 1842. It was replaced 20 years later to make way for the Charing Cross railway bridge – and the Hungerford Bridge chains, of similar design to those proposed for the Clifton bridge, were eagerly snapped up and given a new lease of life in Bristol. Barlow and Hawkshaw modified Isambard's scheme, using three chains instead of two, and widened the roadway from 24ft to 30ft.

In June 1863, a temporary bridge was strung between the two towers, a hugely symbolic achievement in itself.

The last part of the permanent Baltic timber roadway was fixed into position in July 1864, followed by rigorous testing, which saw the bridge carry a spread load of 500 tons of stone, with estimates indicating that it would only fall down if 28,000 tons were laid on it.

Around 150,000 people turned out for the grand opening of the suspension bridge on 8 December 1864, when a huge procession from the city centre, accompanied by the army and 16 bands, marched to the Clifton, where triumphal arches had been erected.

The modified structure as completed is still a definitive showcase of Isambard's vision and talent. Perhaps more importantly, the fact that it was finished posthumously is also a monument to the esteem in which his peers held him, and the strong bonds that he continually forged with Bristol itself.

**ABOVE** A modern-day view of the Wear estuary, with Brunel's North Dock in the top left. It was bought by George Hudson's York, Newcastle & Berwick Railway in 1846, and later became part of the North Eastern Railway. Brunel designed a suspension bridge to span the Wear to carry coal from the south side, but it was never built. North Dock was eclipsed by Sunderland South Docks, when they opened in 1850.

# Chapter 4

# A Head For Steam
## *God's wonderful railway*

Nobody knows for certain who built the first railways. Historians have traced the concept back to ancient Greece, where theatres in Sparta and Megalopolis had mobile buildings used occasionally for performances but which could also be rolled on and off the stage with their wheels following rows of channelled stone rails.

Later a Diolkos, or 'railed way', was built across the 3.7mile-wide Isthmus of Corinth for the long-distance transfer of goods, avoiding the need for a dangerous sea journey around the Peloponnese. Greek historians list eight occasions between 428BC and 30BC when it was used to transport ships across the Isthmus, while the Roman writer Pliny mentioned it carrying wagons.

There is some evidence that the Romans used a very basic form of railway in mines, while horse-drawn systems were certainly in use for industry in Europe by the late Middle Ages.

It is often assumed that railways superseded canals. The reality is that that many horse-drawn tramways in Britain were designed to serve the expanding inland waterways network, which made the Industrial Revolution of the 18th century possible. These tramways took goods to and from the nearest wharf, in cases where it was not practical or affordable to extend the canal.

As already stated, Richard Trevithick, who staged the world's first public demonstration of a steam railway locomotive in 1804, did not foresee the time when the concept would form the basis of a national network of lines linking city to city.

However, while canals and turnpike roads greatly improved transport in many parts of Britain, they were still not capable of satisfying the increasing demands of heavy industry.

The products of the Industrial Revolution – iron and steel in vast quantities, steam-power technology and mass production – made the railway network possible.

The Middleton Railway in Leeds – a heritage line since 1960 – claims to be the world's oldest railway in continuous operation, as it has run ever since it opened in 1758.

In 1801, the Surrey Iron Railway became the first public railway in Britain to be authorised by an Act of Parliament, while the Carmarthenshire Railway at Llanelli, was the second one to be approved. However, despite popular misconceptions to the contrary, it is believed that the Carmarthenshire concern ran trains first.

As previously stated, the Stockton & Darlington Railway became the first public line in the world to be partly operated by steam, when it opened in 1825.

**ABOVE** A colour postcard of a Great Western Railway broad-gauge train hauled at speed by a Rover class locomotive.

**BELOW** Beamish – the North of England Open Air Museum, in County Durham, is a world-leader in terms of research into early steam railways, including the handful that would have been operational during Isambard Brunel's childhood. The museum's replica of a long-lost locomotive type, the six-wheeled 'Steam Elephant', the prototype of which ran at Wallsend Colliery after it was built in 1815, hauls a train comprising wagons typical of the period.

At the time, there was still much debate among early railway promoters as to whether the locomotive was the right way to go: some opted for horse traction, others said cable-hauled trains powered by stationary steam engines would be better.

It was all still very much in the melting pot 25 years after Trevithick's engine successfully ran at Penydarren, the future of railways – if indeed they had one – was still shrouded in uncertainty.

In that year, the directors of the Liverpool & Manchester Railway held the Rainhill Trials in a bid to determine the traction issue, inviting inventors to demonstrate a locomotive that would

be better than those available.

History records that George Stephenson's Rocket beat Timothy Hackworth's, Sans Pareil, and John Braithwaite and John Ericsson's, Novelty to take the £500 prize, and earn the winner a deal to supply locomotive for the line.

The success of the Liverpool & Manchester renewed public interest in trunk railways, and Stephenson's son Robert was appointed engineer-in-chief to build the 112-mile London & Birmingham Railway, which had been authorised in 1833.

City fathers around Britain stood up and took notice: they also wanted the benefits of a steam railway and its rapid connection to the capital.

Dr John Anderson had drawn up the first plan for a railway from Bristol to London in 1800, when only horse traction would have been available. Twenty-four years later, John Louden McAdam, the road builder, promoted the London & Bristol Railroad Company, which would have run through Mangotsfield, Wootton Bassett, Wantage and Wallingford, but with a terminus at Brentford, however this scheme quickly fizzled out.

The opening of the Liverpool & Manchester Railway had a resounding impact nationally, as it proved that steam engines could transport goods and passengers over long distances, in a relatively short space of time. Accordingly, in 1832, two further proposals for a London-Bristol railway were issued, but both failed to raise sufficient capital.

However, in autumn that year, four Bristol businessmen, John and William Harford, Thomas Guppy and George Jones, agreed to pursue the idea and seek support from those with greater influence.

On 21 January 1833, a meeting was held between the Merchant Venturers, who had supported Isambard over the suspension bridge project, Bristol Corporation, the Bristol Dock Company, the Chamber of Commerce and the Bristol & Gloucestershire Railroad Company, to look at the prospect of building a line to London.

Agreement was reached to fund a survey of the route, and appointed none other than Isambard's friend and colleague of the harbour improvement scheme, Nicholas Roch, now a member of the Bristol Docks Committee, to find

ABOVE The coat of arms of the Great Western Railway, which includes the shields of London and Bristol, above an entrance to Paddington station.

an engineer for the job.

On 21 February 1833, Roch told Isambard about the project, and he along with several rivals were invited to survey a route. The winner would be chosen on the basis of whichever project would be cheapest.

Isambard was having none of it.

He told the railway committee that he would only survey a route that was the best, not the cheapest – and gambled with his reputation. He won.

The committee confirmed his appointment, with WH Townsend as his assistant – a local engineer who had designed the horse-drawn Bristol & Gloucestershire Railway, which ran from coal mines at Coalpit Heath to the

ABOVE The National Railway Museum's replica of Stephenson's Rocket and its Liverpool & Manchester Railway train. Although built primarily for the purpose of competing in, and winning, the Rainhill Trials of 1829, Rocket did not play a significant part in traffic on what was the world's first inter-city railway. However, it is generally regarded as marking the watershed between early steam locomotives and 'modern' types, which would be used by Isambard Brunel on his Great Western Railway.

River Avon at Cuckold's Mill.

Isambard was given a month to survey the route and set out on horseback.

After he came up with a preferred line, estimated cost £2,800,000, the project was formally launched at the Bristol Guildhall on 30 July 1833, when it was decided that a company should be formed to build the line, with a general board of management, drawing directors from both Bristol and London.

Two committees were formed, one in each city, and their first joint meeting of the London & Bristol Railroad was held at the offices of Gibbs & Sons in Lime Street, in the City of London, on 22 August 1833.

When the prospectus was issued shortly afterwards, the name Great Western Railway appeared for the first time.

It was estimated that £3-million would be needed to build the line, but by October that year, only a quarter of it had been raised.

Nonetheless, on 7 September, Isambard was told to start work on the detailed survey, and set off again on his horse.

No railway would receive parliamentary sanction unless half its capital had been subscribed, and so on 23 October, the directors announced that they were to build two railways, one from London to Reading with a branch to Windsor, and the other from Bristol to Bath, in the meantime funds would be raised for them to be joined up at a later date.

In March 1834, the Great Western Railway Bill was passed in the House of Commons by 182 votes to 92, but had then to go to committee stage.

The committee, chaired by Lord Granville Somerset, met on 16 April – and then sat for 57 days to discuss the bill.

Objectors had to be heard one by one. It was claimed that passengers would be "smothered in tunnels" and "necks would be broken," and that the water supply for Windsor Castle would be destroyed. A farmer also expressed fears that his cattle would die if they passed under a railway bridge. The provost of Eton College claimed that the railway would be "dangerous to the morals of the pupils."

Isambard took the witness stand for 11 days, and was praised for his patience and skill in answering questions under cross-examination. Ultimately, the committee approved the bill and returned it to the Commons.

It was, however, rejected by the House of Lords on 25 July 1834, by 47 votes to 30 – but by then, the scheme had engendered so much public support that victory for the objectors would be short lived.

The company issued a new prospectus in September 1834, this time for a complete trunk railway running via Bath, Chippenham, Wootton Bassett, Swindon, Wantage, Reading, Maidenhead and Slough, to be built for £2,500,000.

The 116-mile route had the distinct advantage over the shorter and more direct alternative between Bradford-on-Avon, Hungerford and Devizes, because it offered access to Oxford, Cheltenham and the Gloucestershire wool trade, with the growing industrial area of the South Wales coalfield just an extension away.

Company secretary Charles Saunders pulled out all the stops to raise the capital, and announced at the end of February 1835 than £2-million had been raised.

Again, the bill was approved by the Commons and went to committee stage, where it was debated for just 40 days this time, facing opposition from the London & Southampton Railway, which proposed a more direct line to Bath.

The committee returned the bill to the Commons after making a series of concessions, including the proviso that the route should be built no nearer to Eton College than three miles.

The bill received royal assent on 31 August 1835 – and work began within a month.

Isambard Kingdom Brunel's greatest hour had come.

# Chapter 5

# The Railway Adventure Begins
## *Paddington to Swindon*

The building of the Great Western Railway began in 1836, the same year that Isambard Brunel married Mary Horsley, sister of accomplished painter John Callcott Horsley, a member of the Royal Academy, who was later to paint his portrait on several occasions.

The wedding took place on 5 July in Kensington church, followed by a honeymoon in North Wales and the West Country, with GWR company secretary, Charles Saunders, meeting him midway through the trip at Cheltenham, to bring him up to speed on the building of the line.

The couple moved into their stylish home at 18 Duke Street between Piccadilly and Pall Mall (now covered by the Colonial Office), which he had been able to afford on his £2000-a-year salary from the GWR.

They eventually had three children, including one, Henry Marc, who also became an engineer and worked on Tower Bridge, with Beauchamp Tower, inventor of the spherical engine – crossing the Thames in the air while his grandfather had burrowed beneath it.

Isambard's appointment as engineer to the GWR, together with other high-profile projects had finally given him an income on which he felt he could sustain a family; indeed, after work began on the line at both ends, shortly after its enabling act was passed, he rarely had cause to look back in

ABOVE Dawn near Reading, showing a westbound train, circa 1870.

financial terms.

The eventual terminus chosen for the GWR was at a village called Paddington, then a rural location on the outskirts of the city of London.

The first contract for the construction of the line had been let in September 1835 for the building of a stupendous 891ft-long viaduct at Hanwell, across the River Brent in London, comprising eight brick arches with a span of 70ft, the highest being 65ft.

It was named after Lord Wharncliffe, who had helped the GWR bill through the Lords, and it still carries his coat-of-arms today. Originally the viaduct carried two broad gauge tracks, but it was widened in 1890, the extra north pier matching Isambard's original two, and today carries four tracks.

Again, Isambard opted for an Egyptian style for the structure, as with his original Clifton Suspension Bridge plan, mirroring the contemporary trend towards neo-classical architecture.

Indeed, Brunel structures seem designed to appear as if the Romans had never left Britain in 410 AD and had finally laid railways between their temples, villas and amphitheatres in a new golden age.

Daubed with graffiti today, the viaduct nonetheless remains one of the real treasures of the borough of Ealing. However, it was easily eclipsed in magnificence by the semi-elliptical

twin-span bridge cross the Thames at Maidenhead, which remains one of Isambard's finest achievements.

Here, Isambard had been faced with crossing a river, which was a navigable channel and 100ft wide. The river commissioners stoutly refused any obstruction, so Isambard had to design a bridge with only one support in the middle, so it would allow clearance for the barges – whose trade was soon to be killed off by the GWR.

In turn, Isambard refused to raise the level of the railway and interrupt the super-smooth 1-in-1320 ruling gradient between London and Didcot.

Drawing on experience gained in the building of the Thames Tunnel, he came up with a rule-stretching design that had never been attempted before, in order to tackle this extreme wideness.

Critics insisted that the bridge, the

ABOVE Isambard Brunel's early wrought-iron bridge carrying his Windsor branch.

largest brick feature on the London-Bristol line, would never stand up. We are still waiting for them to be proved right.

The bridge too was widened in the 1890s, again to Isambard's design. Isambard later admitted that had it been built 20 years later, he would have used cast iron or timber; had he done so, Maidenhead would have been aesthetically so much poorer and Victorian bridge technology that much more limited.

Despite the fact that Isambard was at the forefront of bridge-building technology and had placed himself at its cutting edge, during the early years of the building of the railway, heavy criticism arose about the questionable state of the track as well as poor locomotive performance.

Isambard found himself having to defend his choice of 7ft 01/4in gauge to hostile shareholders. He survived the criticism, and was allowed to carry on his work.

Nevertheless, it had become clear that while engineer extraordinaire Isambard had dabbled with locomotive design like the Gaz Engine project, there were many who knew much more about steam railway engines.

While the first stages of the railway were being built, Isambard had ordered a motley collection of 19 locomotives from various builders across the country, after giving them the most basic specifications to follow and allowing

**BELOW LEFT** This model, a rare surviving locomotive from the broad-gauge era, is now in the National Railway Museum at York.

**BELOW RIGHT** GWR locomotive engineer Daniel Gooch, pictured with a model 2-2-2 engine, which he commissioned from London craftsman John Clement in 1840.

them to design and produce the rest.

The end results as delivered, were at best patchy in performance, but Isambard realised that his railway career would depend on their success.

A shining knight had already appeared in the summer 1837, in the form of 20-year-old Daniel Gooch, who had written to Isambard about the position of locomotive engineer on the GWR.

We've all heard about cases in tabloid newspapers when a 16-year-old fan applies for the managerial vacancy at a Premiership football club and is sportingly given a guided tour of the ground, and a chance to meet the players, purely for publicity, but of course his application is taken no further.

However, in this case, Gooch had rather more substance to him. When he made his application, he had already worked at Robert Stephenson's Vulcan Foundry in Newton-le-Willows and

helped his brother, TL Gooch, survey the London & Birmingham and Manchester & Leeds railways, with a brief spell of unsuccessful engine-building in Gateshead along the way.

Despite Gooch's tender years, Isambard was so impressed after travelling north to interview him, that he followed his instincts, and gave him the job at £300 per year.

"I was very young to be entrusted with the management of the locomotive department of so large a railway," Gooch later said, "but I felt no fear."

Gooch was entranced by the potential of broad gauge, but was horrified at the sight of some of those early locomotives delivered to the GWR on Isambard's orders, including one built to an absurd design with a 10ft driving-wheel on a 2-2-2 leading truck, and with its boiler mounted on a trailing chassis behind.

While the line was still under construction however, Gooch had time to set up a locomotive building operation for the company and produced workable designs for its future.

In the meantime, after the initial length to Taplow had opened, it became clear that only six of the motley collection of engines ordered by Isambard were capable of running.

Saving the GWR's bacon was none other than Robert Stephenson, who supplied a 2-2-2 locomotive, North Star, which had been built for the 5ft

ABOVE Architect, printer and publisher Charles Cheffins commissioned artist JC Bourne to produce a series drawings of the Great Western Railway. These were printed in The History and Description of the Great Western Railway, published by David Bogue in 1846, and the best depiction of Isambard's pioneering line in its infancy. Wharncliffe Viaduct at Hanwell, was the first major engineering feature on the GWR line from Paddington.

BELOW Wharncliffe Viaduct today.

6in-gauge New Orleans Railway before the order had been cancelled.

Regauged to 7ft 0¼in, North Star arrived at Maidenhead by barge at the end of November 1837 and waited there until track laying reached it in May 1838. Gooch claimed to have played a part in the design of North Star, which was so successful that a sister locomotive, Morning Star, soon followed. They

mile short of the town, at the village of Taplow.

By 1839, the passenger service was extended over Maidenhead Bridge to Twyford, and the GWR board ordered Gooch to design and buy locomotives capable of handling this longer run.

He modified the Stars by introducing the large haystack-style firebox, so typical of broad-gauge engines, along

were so successful that a further ten of the type were bought for the GWR.

The London to Maidenhead section opened to paying passengers on 4 June 1838, although a directors' special had been run five days before, hauled by North Star, when a banquet for 300 guests was held in a tent at Maidenhead. The initial Maidenhead terminus was a

with outside sandwich frames, a domeless boiler covered in wooden planks and inside cylinders. And so Fire Fly, the first of 62 hugely successful 2-2-2 locomotives of the Firefly class, was delivered, quickly relegating the engines ordered by Brunel to the scrapheap.

The GWR had great cause to thank the young upstart and never looked back.

It was the start of a great partnership between Isambard and Gooch, who was by no means a 'yes' man. He would not hesitate to criticise his superior, if he thought it appropriate, even to the GWR board itself, while always holding Isambard in great respect.

The next big obstacle to building the line westwards presented itself in the form of a hill at Holme Park next to the village of Sonning, east of Reading.

At first Isambard planned a mile-long tunnel through it, but then agreements with landowners were reached so that it could be opened out into a cutting, as the GWR board feared that passengers might have been deterred from travelling for so long in the dark.

The monstrous Sonning cutting, one of the biggest excavations of the early railway age, nearly two miles long and up to 60ft deep, took a team of 1200 navvies, aided by 200 horses, to dig out during the summer of 1838.

Not only that, but a court case had been brought against Isambard by a contractor who had been appointed to do several contracts near Bristol. It took 16 years before final judgement was given.

Storms that winter caused horren-

dous delays to the work at Sonning, and it was not until the end of 1839 that the cutting was completed, complete with a brick three-arch bridge to carry the main London-Reading road across it, along with a smaller timber bridge that

ABOVE Sonning cutting was built because the GWR directors were concerned that passengers might be scared of the dark in a mile-long tunnel.

many believe was the basis for the great trestle viaducts that Isambard would build in Devon and Cornwall in the coming years.

Laying broad-gauge track took longer than a conventional railway with sleepers, and so the completion of the GWR exceeded the original completion date. The 30ft 'baulks' laid between each cross-member or 'transom' at 15ft intervals and packed with ballast to form a firm foundation for the base, required far more labour and raw materials, not least of all the need to treat the pine to prevent rot.

Needless to say, this system of laying track, nicknamed the 'baulk road', and its design, was not adopted elsewhere in Britain.

On 14 March 1840, a special directors' train was run from Paddington to Reading – hauled by Fire Fly – and the first public services followed on 30 March, as the company needed to begin earning money without delay.

Reading and Slough were both built as 'one-sided' stations by Isambard, his logic being that the entrance and booking hall should be on the side of the railway where the town lay, so that the public should not have to cross the tracks.

The eastbound (or up) and westbound (down) platforms were arranged so that they would be on the same side, and each accessed by loops off the mainline. There was much criticism of the amount of crossovers that the trains had to make to leave the mainline and enter the loops to pick up or set down passengers, but in those days of comparatively spare traffic, it worked well. Isambard was later to effect the same arrangements at other stations including Taunton, Gloucester, Newton Abbot and Exeter.

As traffic increased and the railway was updated, these one-siders were replaced with conventional stations; Reading was the last to be converted, in 1899.

The section from Reading to

Steventon on the Oxford turnpike road, opened on 1 June 1840, allowing a coach connection to the city 10 miles away, until it was superseded by a station at Didcot in 1844 – a case of an early park-and-ride.

Near Steventon station, Isambard ordered a large Tudor house to be built for the line's superintendent; it was also used as the directors' offices and for their board meetings in the early years.

West of Reading, two more splendid Brunel Thames crossings can be seen, the sweeping brick arches of Basildon Bridge, west of Pangbourne and Moulsford Bridge, just before Cholsey.

Furthermore, the short branch from Slough to Windsor includes the bowstring Brunel's Bridge with its 203ft span. It is the oldest surviving example of one of Brunel's wrought-iron bridges.

It was on 20 July 1840 that services extended to Faringdon Road, 63½ miles from Paddington, later renamed Challow. That remained the terminus for five months, and on 17 December 1840, services were extended to Hay Lane, a minor road crossing at the entrance to Studley cutting, four miles from Wootton Bassett. This temporary terminus was later officially named Wootton Bassett Road.

It was from this date that the GWR issued its first proper passenger time-table. Meanwhile, a sleepy little market town called Swindon three miles back up the line was about to be hauled on to the international stage by Brunel and, in particular, Gooch.

**BELOW** This splendid pub sign, at a hostelry of the same name, near Cholsey, recalls Morning Star, the second of the Robert Stephenson locomotives, which made the early GWR a success.

# Chapter 6

# Temple Meads
## *The first great terminus*

The relatively short Great Western Railway route between Bath and Bristol proved to be fraught with difficulties. While none of them were on anything like the scale of the task of tunnelling through Box Hill, seven tunnels were needed on this section, in addition to numerous deep cuttings and a two-mile-long embankment near Keynsham, not to mention a 28-arch viaduct at Twerton, as the railway left Bath. Furthermore, a short section of the Bristol Avon needed to be diverted near Fox's Wood Tunnel.

The first contract for building work in Bristol itself was placed in March 1836, but difficulties with the contractor and, yet again, prolonged wet weather,

delayed completion by at least a year.

The line between Bristol and Bath opened to the public on 31 August 1840, 10 days after Isambard privately treated some of the directors of the GWR's Bristol committee to the first train trip from there to Bath, behind Firefly class 2-2-2 locomotive Arrow. There was no carriage, so the party had to travel on the locomotive footplate.

When this short section of the trunk route officially opened, more than 5000 passengers were carried on the railway on the first day. Neither city ever had cause to look back.

The Brunel transport revolution continued with the building of Bristol's Temple Meads station. Predating his

**ABOVE** Class 47 diesel
No 47484, named after
Isambard Kingdom
Brunel, heads away
from the 'second
generation' Bristol
Temple Meads station
in July 1985

stylish rebuilt Paddington terminus by nearly 15 years, it set new standard for others to follow in its wake.

Building work at the site – which lay a fair walk away from the city centre – began in 1838. The frontage on Temple Gate was designed in Brunel's grandiose neo-Tudor style, with tall square-headed widows and heavy mullions, to screen the engine and train sheds behind it, which were supported by a series of 44 massive brick-flattened arches at 10ft intervals.

A 74ft single-span hammer beam roof, built entirely from wood, in a direct copy of London's Westminster Hall, covered the 220ft-long train shed and its five broad-gauge tracks.

The GWR boardroom and booking hall occupied the first floor of the offices that were linked to the train shed, with the station superintendent living on the top floor, and the company clerk's quarters on the ground floor.

Members of the Bristol committee, possibly disappointed at the very basic facilities originally provided at the Paddington end of the line, had demanded a terminus with architectural features that were in harmony with other buildings in the ancient port, regardless of higher expense.

A letter was sent to the GWR's London committee arguing that Brunel's stylish design could be implemented for just £90 more than a basic building resembling a workhouse – and members agreed.

At the far end of the station were facilities for locomotive servicing and maintenance, with chimneys to take the excess steam and smoke away. The station also had its own goods depot.

The completed Great Western main line was opened on 30 June 1841, when a directors' special left Paddington at 8am and arrived in Bristol four hours later.

By 1845, the timing for an express train between the two cities was reduced to just three hours – light speed at a time when a stagecoach journey from Bath to London could take days, and comparing favourably to the one hour and 40 minutes taken by today's high-speed trains.

The magnitude of such an achievement can only really be appreciated when you consider the rural and isolated nature of much of Britain at the time. Most towns and village kept their own time, which could vary considerably from that of London. It was only the coming of the railways that allowed standardisation of time across Britain to take place, and eventually facilitated the development of the telegraph system.

The contribution made by railway pioneers like Brunel to the modern world in areas such as this – and so much taken for granted today – was to say the least, immense.

The completion of the GWR opened up all sorts of trade possibilities for Bristolians, who had more reason than ever to be grateful to those Brighton actresses whose 'exertions' had led to Isambard convalescing in Clifton.

Even a decade before, such timings would have been seen as nothing less than a miracle, but now the seeds of the period, known as Railway Mania, had been well and truly sown. Not only had trains as a mode of transport been firmly established, with many of the irrational fears about its effects refuted, but the question now on everyone's lips was – 'how many lines can we build, and how quickly?'

In 1825, there had been just 27 miles of passenger-carrying railway lines in Britain. By 1841, when the GWR opened throughout its 118-mile length, that figure had risen to 1775.

By 1850, it would stand at 6559. Ominously for Brunel and his vision for the future of rail transport, the bulk of that mileage was standard gauge.

In 1845, a second Temple Meads terminus was built, at a right angle to

Brunel's first station building, for use by his 'next' line, the Bristol & Exeter Railway, which was also built to broad gauge.

The Exeter line had arrived in 1842, and at first, vehicles had to be transferred between the two railways by means of turntables where the tracks intercepted; moving a complete train one vehicle at a time would take hours.

Eventually, a curve was laid to link the two lines, and it was served by an express platform by through trains. The Exeter trains, terminating at Bristol meanwhile, had to reverse into the GWR station until the second station was built.

Congestion worsened when the Midland Railway acquired the Brunel broad-gauge Bristol & Gloucester Railway, for a higher price than the GWR was prepared to pay for it – much to the Paddington empire's eternal regret.

**ABOVE** A contemporary drawing of the exterior of Brunel's original Temple Meads station

The Midland Railway also gained the right to run its trains into the GWR Temple Meads station, and standard-gauge rails were added when the Gloucester line was converted to 4ft 8½in gauge in 1854.

In 1871, the three companies finally sat around a table and agreed to pay for a new joint station to be built.

The Bristol & Exeter's train shed was knocked down, and a new station designed by that company's engineer, Francis Fox, was built – right on the curve.

Its distinctive pointed-arched iron roof on lattice ribs was – and still is – 500ft long and 125ft wide. Opened in 1878, it is the stupendous curving Temple Meads that we know today.

Brunel's station original was kept for trains terminating at Bristol, mainly from the Midland line, and Fox doubled its length with a wider and higher pitched light iron roof that joined to the roof of his new station. The two stations came together in a V formation, and Matthew Digby Wyatt designed an entrance building in French Gothic style, to serve both.

More platforms were added in 1935, but outside the curving train shed. However, Rationalisation in 1966, following the Beeching cuts, left platforms 12-15 taken out of use. Brunel's train shed was closed, along with the rest of the terminal portion of the station and the tracks inside it lifted. The extension built by Fox became a car park, and in 1970 shortened to make way for a new power signal box.

Thankfully, the massive historical importance of the Old Station, as Brunel's terminus has come to be known, led to the building being restored and given a new lease of life as the British Empire & Commonwealth Museum.

It has been said that so much of the face of Bristol today has its roots in Brunel and his works, that it would have been unforgivable if this prize asset, on which Bath Spa station was modelled to a large extent, had been allowed to pass into the history books.

# Chapter 7

# Locomotives

## *Steam behemoths of the broad gauge*

Many of the magnificent structures designed and built by Isambard Brunel at the dawn of the railway age, which placed him decades ahead of his contemporaries, have survived the passage of time and are still carrying out their intended functions.

However, even more impressive, at least from a mechanic's point of view, were the steam locomotives that made his Great Western Railway the greatest in the world, but have now all but vanished.

They were truly colossal engines, the like of which we have not seen in regular service for more than a century, similar in concept to, but very different in appearance from, those that many of us remember from the last days of steam on British Railways, or have ridden behind on one of this country's excellent preserved lines.

The Brunel era was the golden age of huge brass domes, stovepipe chimneys, boilers coated with wooden planks and no cab roofs or sides to offer protection to drivers and firemen. With massive over-the-top central driving wheels, the bigger they were, the faster the engine would go.

Isambard's engines were from the days we now regard as pure antiquity, and which we can view only in black-and-white photographs or hand-coloured postcards.

Running on Brunel's 7ft 0¼in broad

gauge, these behemoths, with their ability to haul much wider loads at more efficient speeds, gave the appearance of being a completely different type of transport compared to the rest of the country's 'normal' railways.

What's more, they were world-beaters in every sense. Yes, the broad gauge was Brunel's idea, but it was another young upstart engineering genius who 'fixed it for him' – and saved it from becoming a white elephant.

With the appointment of Daniel Gooch as his locomotive superintendent, Isambard quickly proved himself to be a shrewd recruitment manager, as well as an industrial colossus.

Few would have considered an application for a job of such enormous standing and responsibility from a 20 year old. However, Gooch had placed himself in the right place at the right time, and Isambard was spot on when he picked the Northumbrian to be his sidekick, despite his tender years.

It was to be a truly explosive combination, and one that would greatly advance transport and technology within a short space of time.

Isambard may well have devised a railway system, which to him and his supporters was superior to any other, but it was Gooch who provided the means to run it.

Starting work on the nascent Great Western Railway, Gooch was plunged in at the deep end, having not only to sort out the mechanical problems with the motley collection of prototype locomotives Isambard had hurriedly ordered, but also finding out which ones were capable of hauling trains.

Nonetheless, Brunel and Gooch worked successfully to improve the steaming and reduce the coke consumption of North Star when it became clear that the Stephenson engine was not as efficient as it might be.

At first, North Star could haul no more than 16 tons at 40mph, but following modifications by made by the pair, which included increasing the size of the blast pipe and ensuring that the exhaust steam was discharged up the middle of the chimney, its performance improved to the point whereby it could haul 40 tons at 40mph – while consuming less than a third of the quantity of coke previously used.

It was through work of this ilk that Gooch honed his skills on the sharpest-possible learning curve and, given a unique opportunity by Isambard, became one of the finest locomotive engineers of the 19th century.

The great disappointment with the locomotives supplied from outside manufacturers spurred Gooch to press the GWR to have its own workshops at Swindon where it could build its own.

He shared Isambard's deep conviction that 7ft 0¼in was the real way forward for railways, because the wider trains were, "safer, swifter, cheaper to run, more comfortable for passengers and more commodious for goods."

Improvement work on North Star and its sister locomotives led to the introduction of Gooch's Firefly class, of which seven different outside manufacturers built 62 examples – in just two years. They had a wheel arrangement of 2-2-2 – the middle '2' refers to the driving wheel – which in this case was 7ft in diameter.

Fire Fly, the first of its class, had been delivered on 12 March 1840 and made its debut on 13 days later, hauling two carriages carrying 40 passengers and a truck from Paddington to Reading.

As previously stated, fellow class member Fire Ball worked the first train from Bristol to Bath on 31 August 1840, and Actaeon was used for the opening of the Bristol & Exeter Railway on 1 May 1844.

Gooch also had the honour of driving the first Royal Train, when Queen Victoria travelled on a special from

Slough to Paddington on 13 June 1842, behind his locomotive Phlegethon.

The fact that he drove both trains highlighted that he was not only a brilliant engineer, but also a hands-on engineman too. Therefore, he could with much justification claim to be the father of the express train.

The Firefly class engines were painted with chocolate-brown frames, green wheels with black tyres, vermillion buffer beams – and a green boiler and firebox. This livery evolved into the famous Brunswick green, which became the trademark of the Swindon empire, right up until the end of steam, and was even adopted by British Railways for many of its locomotives built elsewhere.

In trials between broad and standard gauge locomotives, held in 1845 to determine which system was the superior, Firefly-class engine Ixion exceeded 60mph and was able to run from London to Didcot with a 71-ton load at nearly 55mph – clearly far better than anything that 4ft 8½in gauge had to offer. The Gooch engines were more reliable too.

**ABOVE** The National Railway Museum's modern-day replica of Daniel Gooch's Iron Duke, on display outside the Royal Albert Hall in London for the GWR 150th Anniversary. This class of locomotive was the flagship of Brunel's Great Western Railway.

Twelve Fireflys were ferried across the Bristol Channel for use on the new Brunel-designed South Wales Railway in 1850, and they were also employed on the postal service between Paddington and Bristol, introduced on 1 February 1855.

As locomotive design evolved and newer engines with greater capacity were needed to replace them, several Fireflys were rebuilt to soldier on as saddle tanks.

Each of them gave an average of around half a million miles in service, and were so successful that the last one, Ixion, wasn't withdrawn until as late as July 1879.

In 1842, next off the Gooch drawing board were the 21 members of the Sun class, also 2-2-2s, and built by four different outside manufacturers. They were smaller than the Fireflys, with 6ft not 7ft driving wheels, and were less successful, being rebuilt as saddle tanks at the end of the decade, and performing much better in that guise.

Then came the 2-4-0 Leos, of which there were 18. They were the GWR's first purpose-built goods engines. As traffic levels and loads increased, they too were converted to saddle tanks for

lighter duties.

By the time the Hercules class 0-6-0s, the first of this wheel arrangement on the GWR, were delivered in 1842, the company had 136 engines from 11 different makers. Gooch saw that it was inevitable that apart from maintaining them at Swindon Works, which opened the following year, the GWR had to start building its own.

While 0-6-0 goods-locomotive Premier (the first of a class of 12) was built at Swindon Works in February 1846, but because the boiler had been supplied from elsewhere, it cannot be said to have been the first locomotive to be completely constructed by the GWR.

As previously mentioned, the 2-2-2 express passenger engine Great Western was the first to be built there in its entirety – and what a stunning engine it was.

Finished in April 1846, after just three months, and visually similar to the Fireflys, its 8ft-driving wheel allowed it to show the true potential of Brunel broad gauge, running 194 miles from Paddington to Exeter in three hours 28 minutes.

The average speed of nearly 57mph was earth shattering as far as an unsuspecting 1840s public was concerned, turning a journey that took several days by stagecoach, into one that could be

**TOP RIGHT** Dual identity: No 1207 was an Armstrong Standard Goods locomotive designed for 4ft 8 1/2in gauge but running as a Brunel broad-gauge locomotive. The wheels have been placed outside the frames and new splashers added. An old broad-gauge tender has been added, but otherwise few alterations were necessary. While No 1207 was built in August 1876, it was not converted to broad gauge until May 1884, along with nine others of the same type. All were converted back to standard gauge in 1892. It is seen at Taunton on the Bristol & Exeter line performing station pilot duties.

**BOTTOM RIGHT** Bristol & Exeter Railway-built 2-4-0 No 2019 is seen piloting a GWR Rover. No 2019 was built as BER No 8 in June 1872, replacing one of the company's original 4-2-2s.

done in a morning or afternoon.

The locomotive Great Western (as well as the company that built it) set new standards of power and speed, taking the steam engineering work of Trevithick and the Stephensons to a breathtaking new plateau.

However, its big initial drawback was the excess weight over the front carrying wheels, which eventually broke its

leading axle. Gooch modified his design by extending the frames and converting it into an even more successful 4-2-2.

The first class of engines to be built entirely at Swindon were the Princes, six 2-2-2s all with 7ft-driving wheels, apart from the semi-experimental Witch that had a 7ft-6in version, built for passenger work.

While the Princes held the fort on the Paddington-Exeter run for which they had not really been designed, Gooch modified his Great Western design to perfect the class which was to become the broad-gauge flagship, the Iron Dukes, 29 2-2-2s with 8ft-driving wheels.

The GWR broad-gauge classes usually took their name from the first to be built. So, Iron Duke, outshopped from Swindon in April 1847, was so

TOP LEFT North Star was the engine that made Brunel's broads gauge really work, but it was not built by the company. It was delivered to Maidenhead by barge on 28 November 1837. This drawing shows it in its original condition. It was later rebuilt with new cylinders, extended wheelbase and a new boiler. It was preserved at Swindon from January 1871 until February 1906 when it was cut up – by none other than a future locomotive-designing genius in the form of William Stanier. Some parts survived and were incorporated in the replica built in 1925, which is now in STEAM – Museum of the Great Western Railway set up in Isambard Brunel's former works at Swindon.

BOTTOM LEFT Pearson's amazing 4-2-4Ts gave the Brunel-designed Bristol & Exeter Railway the capability at running of speeds up to 81mph. No 2002 is pictured at Bristol following the takeover of the line by the GWR.

called because its trial run took place on 29 April, the Duke of Wellington's birthday. Swindon turned out 22 of the Iron Dukes between then and 1851, while Rothwell and Co at Bolton made another seven in 1854-55.

They really were the ultimate land transport of the day. In 1848, one of the class Great Britain, maintained average speeds of 67mph on its runs from London to Didcot, and regular timetabled trains were maintaining 60mph – impressive even by standards a century later.

Iron Duke ran up 607,412 miles before it was withdrawn in August 1873, while the highest mileage by a sister locomotive was that of Lightning, which reached 816,601 in the 31 years before it was made redundant in 1878.

The most famous engine of the class, the Lord of the Isles, one of the stars of the Great Exhibition of 1851, clocked up nearly 800,000 miles in 30 years with its original boiler.

Gooch, like many locomotive engineers who were to follow him, took great care when it came to boiler design, and rightly considered it to be the heart of the locomotive upon which all else depended.

In 1847, the Pyracmon class six of 0-6-0 freight locomotives, slightly bigger than the Premiers appeared, followed in 1851 by the eight Caesar 0-6-0s. However, the largest class of all in terms of locomotive numbers was Gooch's 'Standard Goods', or Ariadne class, with 102 being built at Swindon in the 11 years from 1852. They were so successful that examples survived right up to the end of broad gauge in 1892.

In 1860, the GWR switched from coke to coal as the fuel for its steam locomotives after succeeding with experiments to burn bituminous coal, which Isambard had begun 20 years earlier.

Both the Brunel broad gauge and Great Western empire had, by then, spread way beyond London-Bristol-Exeter.

Gooch had also designed many successful broad-gauge locomotives for the Bristol & Exeter Railway, the Vale of Neath Railway, the South Devon Railway and the Cornwall Railway as well as the Great Western.

To tackle the notorious inclines on the South Devon between Exeter and Plymouth, he came up with the Corsair 4-4-0 saddle tanks, with a leading bogie axle – then a major innovation in design. A variation of these was supplied to the Neath line for tackling the daunting Glyn Neath bank.

While the BER was independent from

the GWR, it built its own locomotives at Bristol. There, the line's own locomotive superintendent James Pearson, who had worked under Isambard on his initial South Devon scheme as described in the next chapter, designed a type whose spectacular performances easily gave Gooch more than a run for his money.

Rothwell & Co at Bolton built Pearson's incredible 4-2-4 tank engines,

LEFT Imagine if, in many centuries to come, all that survived of the world's motorcar industry was a Mini pick-up truck. In the South Devon Railway museum at Buckfastleigh, pride of place goes to Tiny, the sole-surviving Brunel broad-gauge engine, in its complete and original form - and it was not even built for his Great Western Railway. Built by Swan & Co, Plymouth, in 1868, it may well have been the smallest engine ever to run on broad gauge. Running on four coupled wheels, it had a vertical boiler and was designed to replace horse traction on the original South Devon Railway, Sutton Harbour branch, in Plymouth. It later became a shunter in Newton Abbot yard. It was withdrawn in June 1883 and preserved as a static exhibit in the town's railway works.

BELOW Great Britain, one of the Iron Duke class of 4-2-2s, which blazed a trail for steam at speed, and which were the most famous engines of all on Brunel's broad gauge. The Iron Dukes were eventually replaced by the Rover class, which were supposedly a 'renewal' or rebuild of the earlier locomotives. While the Rovers were called 'renewals', and carried the names of the Iron Dukes that they replaced, it is believed that only the first three contained parts salvaged from the earlier engines, and the other 21 were completely new.

with their 9ft-driving wheels, in 1853-54. Numbered 39 to 46, they were used on express trains including the 'Flying Dutchman', and became the fastest of their kind in the country; one reaching 81.8mph while running down the same Wellington bank where City of Truro was claimed to have touched 102.3mph in 1904.

In 1855 came the class of 10 Waverleys built by Robert Stephenson & Co in Newcastle. They were the only 4-4-0 tender locomotives to run on the broad gauge, and were mainly allocated to Swindon for working services to South Wales, Gloucester and Bristol.

As well as the BER, GWR slowly took over, or absorbed many other lines,

including systems built to standard gauge.

Gooch eventually and reluctantly accepted the fact that the 'superior' 7ft 01⁄4in gauge system's days were numbered – and set his skills to designing standard-gauge locomotives as well.

His last class designed for the GWR was the Metropolitan 2-4-0 broad-gauge tank engines, of which 22 were built between 1862 and 1864.

These were the only GWR broad gauge engines to have outside cylinders and were designed to work over the Metropolitan Railway, which effectively extended the Brunel empire until 15 March 1869, when the broad-gauge and mixed-gauge running rails were removed from its system. These locomotives were fitted with condensing apparatus to nullify the discharge of steam in the tunnels of what would become an integral part of the future London Underground system.

Its critics eventually brought down the broad gauge system. Yet broad gauge or not, there is little dispute that Gooch's designs had been at the leading edge of locomotive design, and provided the motive power that made Isambard's ever-expanding railway

empire work so impressively.

Gooch stood down in September 1864, after years of frustration with the GWR board following a lengthy dip in its financial fortunes.

In all, a total of 407 broad-gauge and 98 standard-gauge locomotives were built to his designs, around half of them in the new town he had created at Swindon.

While had he begun his distinguished career as Isambard's lieutenant, Gooch ended up with a far bigger fortune and a much greater social standing.

A Freemason, he was awarded a baronetcy for his work in laying the first transatlantic cable in 1865 – ironically, as we will see, using a great ship

designed by Isambard – a feat which in many circles acquired him greater fame than his railway work.

He served as a Conservative MP for Cricklade from 1865 until 1885 – yet never made a speech in the House of Commons.

Perhaps more importantly, in 1865 he became chairman of the GWR – a position that Isambard had never managed to reach. During his reign, Swindon Works was again expanded, and under his leadership, the GWR recovered from its financial doldrums.

While his locomotive designs were eventually bettered, and broad gauge passed away, in many ways Gooch laid the foundation for the GWR to grow into one of the Big Four railway companies in Britain, after the Grouping of 1923 – and one of the most widely respected around the globe, a byword for class and quality.

The Times issued daily bulletins on Gooch's health in the days leading up to his death at his luxurious home at Clewer Park, Windsor, in 1889. No other British locomotive engineer would receive such public honour and prestige.

After his death his estate was valued at £750,000 – almost 10 times the

**LEFT** Vulcan was one of the better of the locomotives ordered by for Isambard Brunel's new Great Western Railway, before Daniel Gooch designed his own. Vulcan was built by Charles Tayleur & Co of Newton-le-Willows as a 2-2-2 well tank with 8f driving wheels. It was delivered to the GWR at West Drayton on 25 November 1837. Vastly inferior to the Star class, let along the Fireflys or Iron Dukes, it was the first engine to steam on the GWR, running over a short length of line near Iver in Buckinghamshire on 28 December 1837. It was withdrawn from service as early as 1843, converted to a back tan, re-entered service and clocked up a total of 171,801 miles before final withdrawal in april 1868. It refused to lie down and die, being used as a stationary boiler at Reading until July 1870.

amount left by Isambard and equivalent to about £50-million in today's terms.

His name lives on in Swindon today in Gooch Street, near the railway line, and the Sir Daniel Arms pub in Fleet Street, which lies near his railway village.

Joseph Armstrong, under whom just 70 more broad-gauge engines would be built, replaced Gooch as locomotive superintendent.

Armstrong's Hawthorn class of 26 2-4-0 tender engines with 6ft-driving wheels, some of which were later converted to saddle tanks, also lasted until the end of the broad-gauge era.

Under Armstrong, the Swindon class of 14 0-6-0 goods engines appeared in 1865-66 and eight years later all were sold to the Bristol & Exeter, returning when the GWR absorbed that company in 1874.

The only side tanks to be built for the GWR broad gauge were the six Sir Watkin class 0-6-0s which appeared at the same time, and were at first also fitted with condensing gear for use on the Metropolitan Railway. Three were sold to the South Devon Railway in 1872, and all six were rebuilt as saddle tanks.

Last of all came the 24 Rover class 4-2-2s, based closely on the Iron Dukes, but having vacuum brakes on both the driving and trailing wheels. Here, it should be mentioned that the Iron Dukes had brakes only on the side of the tender, and none at all on the engine. What would our 21st-century health-and-safety obsessed state have made of that?

Rover, one of three fitted in 1888 with bigger boilers, set the mileage record for the class, clocking up a total of 787,174 between 1871 and 1892.

When, after Isambard's death, it became clear that the broad gauge would become extinct sooner rather than later, GWR had the vision to construct engines which could be converted, if necessary, to run on 4ft 8½in gauge.

A total of 112 were built at Swindon, beginning in late 1878 with 10 Armstrong 0-6-0 saddle tanks. They were nothing less than a standard-gauge design adapted with double frames to run on 7ft 0¼in track, and from hereon, the GWR produced no more exclusive broad-gauge designs.

As the older broad-gauge engines were withdrawn as life expired, they were gradually replaced by 'convertibles'.

Armstrong died in June 1877 and was replaced by his assistant William Dean, who designed and produced 41 convertibles at Swindon, the final batch being 20 0-4-2 passenger saddle tanks which proved somewhat unstable and were afterwards converted into 4-4-0 tender engines.

The steam locomotive now reigned supreme, having replaced the horse as the most effective means of land transport. Yet its dominance was not always assured.

Back in the 1840s, and flying in the

face of strong advice from Gooch, Isambard began to wonder whether the steam locomotive really was the be all and end all that the GWR and Bristol & Exeter system had indicated that it was. Forever eager to embrace new ideas, he started looking for the next transport revolution, and saw it beyond the conventional railway.

His vision was, as we shall now see, a main line without any kind of locomotive at all.

**ABOVE** Broad gauge Hawthorn class 2-4-0 Dewrance was built by the Avonside Engine Company in July 1865 and lasted until May 1892. It is seen attached to a mail van – allocated to Plymouth, it was often used on Ocean Mails to Bristol.

# Chapter 8

# Brunel's Second Paddington

## *The ultimate Great Western station*

The phenomenal success of Isambard Brunel's London-to-Bristol railway was such that both termini had to be replaced to cope with greater traffic.

As previously stated, the original scheme included in the Great Western Railway Act of 1835, involved sharing Euston with the London & Birmingham Railway. That was scuppered by a row over land at Camden and Euston, and GWR's movement towards adopting broad gauge.

In July 1837, parliamentary permission was given to build four miles of new line from Acton, to a location next to the Paddington Canal.

The first GWR Paddington station in Bishop's Road was most likely built 'on the cheap' while Isambard awaited sufficient funds to build a far grander design. Its four platforms and plain, wooden-arched, truss-roofed train shed, open to the elements at both sides, was very different from the exquisite terminus he had built at Bristol.

By the late 1840s, the old station was hopelessly outdated, yet the GWR board was reluctant to approve its replacement.

By the end of the railway mania years in 1847, company share values had plummeted. The GWR had to face down angry shareholders in 1849 and tell them that their dividend was being cut from four per cent to two.

However, the directors knew that the

station was becoming hopelessly inadequate, and could lose the company business. In late 1850, they changed their minds, and on 21 December, gave Isambard the green light to build a main terminus worthy of both the capital and the GWR. Needless to say, he had already been making preliminary sketches in anticipation of that inevitable decision.

Isambard's design for Paddington, mark two, which was between Praed Street and Eastbourne Terrace, included a train shed 700ft long and 238ft wide, with 10 tracks, five to serve platforms and five to store stock. Consisting of three spectacular, wrought iron, arched, roof spans, it was supported by two rows of cylindrical, cast-iron columns.

Much of Isambard's inspiration for the new terminus was drawn from the 'glasshouse technology' of Joseph Paxton's Crystal Palace, in which the Great Exhibition of 1851 had been held. Brunel's friend, Matthew Digby Wyatt designed the ironwork for the ornate glass screens at the west end of the station, while Paxton's 'patent glazing' was utilised for the roof lights.

The first train departed from the new station on 16 January 1854, when work on the main roof was still being finished. The new arrival side was finally brought into use on 29 May.

On 5 December 1850, the GWR board took on board a suggestion from

**ABOVE** Paddington station has been altered many times since it was opened in 1854, but the triple-roof span is still an awesome tribute to its designer, Isambard Brunel, and the phenomenal success of the line to Bristol, which necessitated the replacement of the inferior original.

director George Burke that a luxury hotel should be built to serve - and complement – the magnificent new terminus.

The completion of the GWR route from Oxford to Birmingham had, for the first time, placed the company in direct competition with the successor to the London & Birmingham Railway – the London & North Western Railway.

The rival company had opened a pair of hotels at Euston in 1839, and the GWR knew only too well that it could not afford to fall behind.

The Great Western Royal Hotel, as it was named, was the first in the capital to be designed as a major architectural statement, and marked a crucial development in the style and opulence of hotel architecture.

Philip Charles Hardwick drew up plans in the French renaissance style of Louis XIV – the huge mansard roof between corner towers creating a chateau-like impression. The building was also the first significant example in Britain, of what became known as the Second Empire style.

The hotel was opened on 8 June 1854 by Prince Albert, husband of Queen Victoria, and his guest the King of Portugal.

Having 112 bedrooms and 15 sitting rooms, plus lounges, public rooms and restaurants, the Great Western Royal Hotel was hailed as the "largest and most sumptuous hotel in England." It set new standards for accommodation in Britain, in terms of size, comfort and amenities for guests.

The design of the second Paddington station served GWR for more than 40 years, justifying Isambard's efforts.

Traffic continued to grow, however, and removing some of the stock sidings and adding extra platforms, expanded the station's capacity.

While mixed gauge had been rejected at Euston, it became the norm at Paddington in 1861, when the first standard-gauge rails were laid in the

LEFT A commemorative plaque at Paddington honours Brunel

station. They served the lines leading to the West Midlands, which had become part of the expanding GWR empire.

Paddington was linked by a footbridge to Bishop's Road station, which served the Metropolitan Railway's line into the City of London, which opened in 1863.

BELOW GWR 4-4-0 No 3440 City of Truro stands at Paddington after arrival from Derby in May 1992.

FAR RIGHT The platform layout at Paddington on Brunel's blueprint.

That line was worked at first by the GWR as broad gauge – and was the easternmost extremity of the 7ft 0¼in gauge empire. However, it was soon taken over entirely by the Metropolitan, with whom the GWR then built the Hammersmith & City line.

Modifications to Isambard's original design have included station offices in 1881, additional departure platforms in 1885, and more arrival platforms in 1893.

Isambard's station needed updating once more in the early 20th century, when the route to the West Country was shortened by the building of 'cut-off' lines, Fishguard Harbour proved to be a major new gateway to Ireland and new powerful locomotives, designed by George Jackson Churchward, all combined to create a phenomenal expansion of traffic.

Brunel's second Paddington station

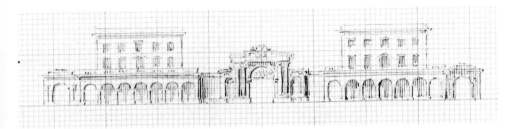

could not cope, and so a new roof span, built from steel instead of wrought iron, was completed in 1915, the year before yet more platforms were built.

Further expansion of Paddington took place between the two world wars, with the GWR drawing on government funds to alleviate unemployment during the depression, in order to modernise the station. The platforms were extended and a new concourse provided.

During the remodelling, the once-separate Metropolitan Bishop's Road station lost its separate identity and was absorbed into the main station.

By 1939, Paddington offered some of the finest passenger facilities anywhere in the country.

It took a pounding during WWII, with more than 400 incidents, although thankfully, there was only one major

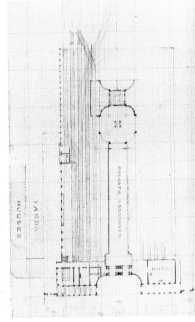

hit, when a 500kg Nazi bomb broke one of the roof ribs in 1944.

Only after the end of steam on British Railways were more major improvements made to Paddington, including, in the late 1980s, the complete restoration of Isambard's triple-span roof, which took several years to complete. Needless to say, it led to a tremendous improvement in its appearance, and thankfully much of the ambience of the 1854 station and its companion hotel can again be appreciated today.

# Chapter 9

# Broadening Horizons
## *Brunel's GWR empire expands*

At one stage, Isambard Brunel had toured the country looking for work. By the 1830s, offers were coming at him from all directions.

Not only had he been placed in charge of turning the Great Western dream into reality, but other new railway companies were also clamouring for his services.

He was given the job of engineer to the Cheltenham & Great Western Union Railway, which held its first meeting in September 1835. He surveyed a route through Stroud and the Chalford Valley, but due to initial opposition – not least of all from the Thames & Severn Canal, the route of which his planned line followed – and the company's inability to raise sufficient finance, the Swindon-Cirencester section was built first.

Leased to the GWR to save buying engines and rolling stock, the new broad gauge railway's Swindon-Cirencester section opened on 31 May 1841. With an eye on a route to the South Wales coalfields, the GWR stumped up the additional capital to finish the route to Cheltenham on 12 May 1845.

Completed at last – but problems were just beginning for Isambard, for at Cheltenham, his line from Swindon met the standard gauge Birmingham & Gloucester Railway. The two companies eventually agreed to share a line between Cheltenham and Gloucester, and a rail

was laid between the 7ft 0¼in gauge tracks to allow 4ft 8½in gauge trains to run along them. This was the first example of mixed gauge on a main line.

A simple enough solution? No way, for at Gloucester, what became known as the Battle of the Gauges broke out. On a basic level, this was simply about the inconvenience of both passengers and freight having to switch trains where Brunel's broad gauge ended and standard gauge began, for apart from mixed gauge sections, there could be no through working. The interchange depot at Gloucester never managed to cope in the way that Brunel promised it would; it caused frequent delays of more than five hours and disruption to the tranship-

ment of freight, all of which were seized upon by critics of the broad gauge.

Another company that took on Isambard as engineer was the Bristol & Gloucester Railway, which he persuaded to adopt 7ft 0¼in gauge rather than the originally planned standard gauge. However, this line joined forces with the Birmingham & Gloucester Railway in January 1845, and the pair became the Bristol & Birmingham Railway.

The new joint concern wanted the GWR to extend broad gauge via its route to Birmingham, but talks broke down, and rivals Midland Railway then bought the Bristol & Birmingham.

Not only did it end Isambard's dream of Birmingham to Bristol broad gauge,

**ABOVE** Isambard Brunel's tubular suspension bridge for the South Wales Railway across the River Wye at Chepstow, provided a direct rail link to London.

but left Gloucester as a permanent break of gauge, and in doing so cast doubts on the long-term survival of the 7ft 0¼in system.

In 1844, Isambard surveyed the route for the projected Oxford, Worcester & Wolverhampton Railway and another from Oxford to Rugby via Banbury, both of which were to be broad gauge. The plans meant penetrating deep into the heart of the territory of GWR's rivals – the London & Birmingham Railway, which opposed them and came up with alternative routes of its own.

A panel of five commissioners of the Board of Trade met to decide which of the opposing schemes should be allowed to proceed, and after first taking a stand against broad gauge, eventually supported it.

In early 1845, broad gauge critic Richard Cobden MP, persuaded the House of Commons to consider the need for a uniform gauge across Britain's railway network to be investigated by a Royal Commission.

Isambard gave evidence on 25 October 1845, answering 200 questions, and said that if he had his time all over again, he would still choose broad gauge, despite severe criticism from fellow railway pioneers like Robert Stephenson.

He was also asked why, when he was appointed engineer of the Taff Vale Railway in 1836, as well as taking a key role in the construction of a line from Turin to Genoa in Italy, he had allowed those lines to be built to standard gauge if he was convinced that 7ft 0¼in was superior. He said that in both cases, the higher speeds, which were then a distinct advantage of broad gauge, were not a priority.

Isambard persuaded the commissioners to hold a series of tests to measure the performances of locomotives of both gauges against each other. This event became known as the Gauge Trials, and was a turning point in British railway history.

As previously mentioned, a Daniel Gooch Firefly 2-2-2, Ixion, easily outperformed a Stephenson 'long boiler' standard-gauge engine, No 54, which even derailed during one test run.

The commissioners retired to consider their verdict, which they delivered in 1846.

They acknowledged that Brunel's gauge was superior to 4ft 8½in, in terms of speed, safety and passenger

convenience, and praised the design of his railways.

However, they said these factors mattered less than the general commercial traffic needs of the country, and in terms of nationwide freight shipment, standard gauge was better.

Could their verdict have been anything but biased against hard facts as presented by Isambard? At the time of the trials, there were just 274 miles of broad-gauge railway, but 1901 of standard gauge. It was so much more convenient and cost effective to let VHS win the day, and sound the death knell for V2000. Needless to say, Isambard was furious.

In July 1846, Parliament passed 'an Act for the Regulating of Railways', stipulating the new lines should be standard gauge, except where any future Act empowering a particular line gave special powers to choose a different width between the rails.

The short and medium-term message to Isambard was simple: carry on building broad gauge. But in the longer term… He then turned his attention to the 90-mile Oxford, Worcester & Wolverhampton Railway, which now had the green light as a broad-gauge route.

The construction of this route became fraught with difficulties; not least of all the company's financial difficulties, but more spectacularly, an incident, which became known as the Battle of Mickleton Tunnel.

During the boring of the tunnel beneath the Cotswold Hills, near Chipping Campden, Isambard became involved in a dispute with the contrac-

ABOVE Isambard Brunel meets Irish 5ft 3in broad gauge: Great Southern & Western Railway J15 class 0-6-0 No 186 rounds Bray Head with a Railway Preservation Society of Ireland special from Dublin to Waterford on 12 May 2005. The tunnel in the distance is on Brunel's original Waterford, Wexford, Wicklow & Dublin Railway alignment, since replaced by a longer tunnel further inland because of serious coastal erosion.

tors, Robert Mudge-Marchant, over payment.

Despite being warned by magistrates that he would be causing a breach of the peace, on 17 July 1851, Brunel arrived at the tunnel site with an army of navvies to evict the contractor – the Riot Act had to be read to ensure peace.

Brunel was back the next day with more navvies, and a series of fights broke out, though not on the scale that the authorities had feared. He won the day, and forced the contractor to reach a settlement.

However, during a national recession, funds for building the line fell short, leaving shareholders angry at GWR's failure to invest sufficient capital to make up the shortfall. Eventually, it was opened in stages – but as a standard-gauge line, and with help from GWR's rivals the Midland Railway and the London & North Western Railway. After several legal battles, in 1858 GWR gave up its insistence that a broad-gauge rail be laid on the route; five years later it became absorbed into the Paddington empire as the West Midland Railway.

By 1858, the Old Worse and Worse (the Oxford, Worcester and Wolverhampton) as it was known, may not have mattered, for GWR broad-gauge trains were by then able to run to Birmingham by a more direct route from Paddington. A mixed-gauge line, authorised in 1846 as the Birmingham & Oxford Junction Railway, opened in 1852, placing it in direct competition with the London & North Western, which by then included the route of the London & Birmingham Railway from Euston.

The GWR's successful march to Birmingham began on 12 June 1844 when it opened a 12-mile branch from Didcot to Oxford, having amalgamated with the scheme's promoter, the Oxford Railway, 33 days previously.

The Oxford & Rugby Railway was promoted at a public meeting on 18 May 1844, attended by several top GWR officials, including Isambard. He argued in vain that the line should first be built to Birmingham, not Rugby.

The Oxford & Rugby received its enabling Act of Parliament the following year, and work started on 4 August 1845.

The Rugby option was eventually discarded in an attempt to reduce opposition from rival companies to GWR schemes elsewhere, and so the line proceeded north to Banbury, to which trains first ran on 2 September 1850, reaching Fenny Compton on 1 October 1852.

A scheme to build a Birmingham & Oxford Junction Railway and associated lines to Wolverhampton and Dudley received Royal Assent on 3 August 1846, but legal wrangling meant that it would be two years before final approval was given for the work to start under the GWR, which had acquired these concerns. The same empowering Act also allowed the GWR to lay broad-gauge rails as well as standard gauge on these lines.

In Birmingham, the station was earmarked for a site at Snow Hill, being reached from the edge of the city centre at Moor Street by way of a deep cutting, which was then covered over to form Snow Hill tunnel, with the land on top sold for development. At first a basic wooden shed was provided as a station, before it was taken down and re-erected at Didcot as a humble carriage depot. A much bigger replacement was built in 1871.

The Birmingham & Oxford also opened to passengers on 1 October 1852, the day after a directors' special

**LEFT TOP** The sole-surviving building from the Isambard Brunel era at Briton Ferry Dock is this tower at the entrance. Local authorities have now assembled a funding package to investigate the possibility of restoring the dock.

**LEFT MIDDLE** As well as the magnificent viaducts in the Chalford Valley, Isambard Brunel also built Stroud station, which includes his office dating from 1845, now Grade II listed, and the nearby goods shed, which is afforded similar protection.

**LEFT BOTTOM** The extraordinary Jackdaw Bridge in the Golden Valley near Stroud, was built by Brunel in 1845 as an means of carrying an inclined plane over his Cheltenham & Great Western Union Railway. The plane lowered stone from Jackdaw Quarry over the railway and on to barges on the Thames & Severn Canal below.

# BROADENING HORIZONS - BRUNEL'S GWR EMPIRE EXPANDS

**RIGHT** GWR extent of Broad Gauge in the late 1860's.

**Reference**
— 7'.0" (BROAD) GAUGE
— MIXED GAUGE
— STANDARD GAUGE

0  10  20  30  40  50 Miles

LITTLE BOOK OF **BRUNEL**

had been run over the 129 miles from Paddington, behind Daniel Gooch's Lord of the Isles – then just three months old, and fresh from the Great Exhibition.

By the time the train reached Aynho, it was half an hour late. As a result, the crew of a mixed-goods train who were uncoupling wagons were unaware of its approach.

The crew finally heard the special, and the driver tried to pull away, but snapped a coupling and left all of his carriages and wagons behind. A collision was inevitable, the special was derailed, but nobody was seriously injured, and the directors completed their journey the following day.

The first Paddington-Birmingham expresses were scheduled to complete the 120-mile journey at an average speed of 47mph.

The broad gauge was subsequently extended from Birmingham to Wolverhampton, but no further. Wolverhampton remained its north-ernmost extremity, dashing Isambard's ambitions to extend to Holyhead and run an Irish Mail service.

He would, however, reach Ireland another way. On 4 August 1845, the South Wales Railway was approved by Parliament, and guess who was appointed engineer?

Plans to continue the Cheltenham & Great Western Union Railway from Gloucester to Fishguard via Chepstow were scuppered as it was refused permission to build a bridge across the tidal River Severn between Frampton-on-Severn and Awre because of Admiralty concerns about ships needing to pass beneath.

Work began in 1848, concentrating, because of financial restraints, on the 75-mile Swansea-Chepstow section, which included a 742-yard tunnel at Newport and huge timber viaducts at Landore (1760ft) and Newport. This section opened on 18 June 1850, with GWR operating the line, built to broad gauge and detached from the rest of the system.

It did, however, link up with the aforementioned 24-mile Taff Vale Railway, which had opened in 21 April 1841, and resisted attempts to convert it to broad gauge, although a mixed-gauge link line was built from the South Wales Railway's Cardiff station to the Taff Vale at Bute Road.

The GWR then gained approval for

a nominally independent Gloucester & Dean Forest Railway to link the South Wales Railway to the Cheltenham & Great Western Union Railway. This line, leased to the GWR, opened on 19 September 1851, but a bridge over the River Wye at Chepstow was needed to link it to the South Wales Railway.

Isambard provided a magnificent structure at a cost of £77,000. Its main 300ft span from a 100ft-high limestone cliff, supported by a 9ft-diameter overhead semi-circular tube girder and cast-iron columns, filled with concrete and sunk in the bed of the river, was followed by three further 100ft spans, all of which stood at 50ft above the high-tide level.

It was a new type of bridge construction, a bespoke solution for a unique location, which typified Isambard's genius and also ended up being a trial run for one of his greatest engineering feats, the Royal Albert Bridge at Saltash, as we shall see.

Trains were able to run from Gloucester to Swansea for the first time on 18 April 1853. It brought Swansea to within six hours of London; the previous best was 15 hours, using stagecoach, a ferry and GWR from Bristol. The line, which used Gooch Firefly locomotives at the start, was extended from Landore near Swansea to Carmarthen on 11 October 1852, with a 789-yard tunnel at Cockett.

In 1844, Isambard had informed the Dublin & Kingstown Railway, the first in Ireland, of his intention to build a broad-gauge line to Fishguard and start a new sea route to Rosslare. His suggestion to help the DKR build a line to Wexford, led to the formation of the Waterford, Wexford, Wicklow & Dublin Railway, work finally beginning on the line from Dublin to Wicklow in August 1847.

By 10 July 1854, the line to Bray was opened. However, serious engineering problems were encountered on the line at Bray Head to the south, where the topography proved difficult for the building of a railway. The coastal route

**LEFT & FAR LEFT** One of the real delights of rediscovering Isambard Brunel's much-varied works is finding little gems that are never mentioned in the same league as Clifton Suspension Bridge or Box Tunnel. Creamy Bath stone was used to build Bradford-on-Avon station on the Wilts, Somerset & Weymouth Railway in Brunel's Tudor station. The Grade II listed building was recently restored.

**BOTTOM LEFT** The all-encompassing train shed was a delightful feature of Isambard Brunel's railways, but the sole survivor on the national network is this splendid Grade II listed example at Frome, designed by JR Hannaford and still in daily use. Timber was used for economy.

had been chosen because it offered spectacular scenery, unlike the more straightforward route inland.

Isambard used his experience from Thames Tunnel days to chisel through the hard rock and build three tunnels to carry the line, which reached Wicklow Town in 1855.

In Wales, Brunel never did reach Fishguard with his broad gauge and instead looked at the west coast of Pembrokeshire for an Irish terminal.

Pressing on, Haverfordwest was reached by the South Wales Railway on 2 January 1854, and Neyland – subsequently renamed Milford Haven and then New Milford – on 1 July 1857.

In the meantime, GWR helped other schemes to intensify the broad-gauge links to South Wales. The Hereford,

Ross & Gloucester Railway linked with the Cheltenham & Great Western Union Railway at Grange Court at one end, and the standard gauge Shrewsbury & Hereford Railway at the other.

Several broad-gauge routes appeared in the Forest of Dean – then a hive of heavy industry because of its coal reserves. They included the Forest of Dean Railway, linking Cinderford to Bullo Cross on the Cheltenham & Great Western Union Railway, the horse-worked Severn & Wye Railway from Coleford to Lydney, the short Forest of Dean Central Railway from Brimspill to the Howbeach Valley.

Isambard was never short of work in South Wales. He engineered the broad-gauge Vale of Neath Railway, which opened between Neath and Aberdare on 24 September 1851, extending from Aberdare to Gelli Tarw, the junction for Merthyr Tydfil, on 2 November 1853. Excelling himself again, Isambard oversaw the construction of a 2495-yard tunnel at Merthyr, plus major viaducts at Merthyr and Werfa.

He also engineered the freight-only South Wales Mineral Railway, which ran from Briton Ferry along the Afan Valley to Glyncorrwg, and not only

had 1-in-22 gradients and a 1109-yard tunnel at Glfylchi, but an ingenious rope-worked incline.

Isambard was engaged in 1851 to design and build a Bristol-style floating dock at Briton Ferry for the shipment of coal, and diverted the River Neath in order to provide a site for it. He built a half-mile broad-gauge extension to the Vale of Neath Railway to serve a wharf at Briton Ferry, opening in 1852, nine years before the dock was completed.

In the far west of Wales, the broad gauge pushed on, part of the Carmarthen Railway being built to 7ft 0¼in gauge for seven miles between Carmarthen and Convil (much of this section is now preserved as the Gwili Railway) and opening on 1 July 1860. Also, the four-mile Milford Railway, which ran between the South Wales Railway at Johnston and Milford Haven docks, was opened on 7 September 1873 and operated by the GWR.

The broad gauge in South Wales, however, did not work to the advantage of the GWR, which had more than a finger in the pie of all the railway schemes in the region that had adopted 7ft 0¼in.

The booming South Wales coalfield

became a labyrinth of independent lines, mainly standard gauge, for conveying coal to docks. Because transhipment to broad-gauge wagons would incur extra labour costs and delays, it was not a preferred option, and comparatively little coal was conveyed on the Brunel system. Meanwhile, rival standard-gauge companies like the Midland Railway and London & North Western began extending into the region.

The GWR had to react to market pressures, in short, by the end of 1872, the entire route from Gloucester to Milford Haven had been converted to standard gauge, with the adjacent broad-gauge lines following suit.

In the meantime, GWR had also been expanding its interests in the south of England, either directly promoting new lines, or investing in and influencing them as independent but 'satellite' concerns.

The mid-1840s Railway Mania saw the 39-mile Berks & Hants Railway built, under Isambard's auspices from the GWR main line at Reading to Hungerford via Newbury, opening on 21 December 1847, and from Southcote Junction to Basingstoke, opening on 1 November 1848.

Simultaneously, the Wilts, Somerset & Weymouth Railway, leaving Isambard's original GWR main line at

Thingley Junction near Chippenham, was opened in stages from 5 September 1848 to 20 January 1857, running via Yeovil and Dorchester. It had branches from Warminster to Salisbury and from Frome to Radstock, (the latter currently the subject of a protracted and stalled preservation scheme), and an offshoot, the Bridport Railway, from Maiden Newton to Bridport, opened on 12 November 1857, and eventually carrying on (after conversion to standard gauge) to West Bay.

The Somerset Central Railway between Highbridge and Glastonbury, engineered not by Brunel but by

Charles Hutton Gregory, was opened on 17 August 1854 as a broad-gauge line worked by the Bristol & Exeter Railway, quickly extending to Wells and Burnham-on-Sea, but much to the anger of the GWR, was converted to mixed gauge after 1861 when the operator's lease expired. This line linked up with the standard-gauge Dorset Central Railway to form, on 1 September 1862, the Somerset & Dorset Railway.

The East Somerset Railway today is a preserved line based at Cranmore, near Shepton Mallet. It is, however, part of a much longer route opened from Witham on the Wilts, Somerset & Weymouth Railway to Shepton Mallet on 9 November 1858 as broad gauge, extending to Wells in 1862 and linking to the Bristol & Exeter's Cheddar branch. The East Somerset was bought by the GWR in 1874.

The Exeter & Crediton Railway was built to broad gauge as it linked to the Bristol & Exeter, but when it was finished in 1847, the London & South Western Railway used its majority shareholding to insist it was converted to standard gauge. The Government's Railway Commission ruled that was illegal, and the line was then leased to the BER. It connected to the North Devon Railway to Barnstaple, which was also broad gauge.

Following complaints that the BER was not managing the line properly, it was leased to the LSWR, which promptly installed mixed-gauge rails, and broad-gauge operations north of Crediton, where the Brunel station office survives today, ceased after 1877.

Meanwhile, another broad-gauge line reached Barnstaple in the form of the Devon & Somerset Railway from Taunton, which was worked by the BER but was not formally taken over by the GWR until 1901.

There were other smaller concerns. In 1857, Royal Assent was given for the broad gauge Dartmouth & Torbay Railway, with Isambard as engineer. Opening at the beginning of August it effectively extended the South Devon Railway, which operated the line, from its Torquay station at Torre to Kingswear, opposite Dartmouth, which was reached by means of a floating bridge or road-vehicle ferry, as it still is today. A typical station booking office building at Dartmouth was opened in 1889 – but it has never been physically served by trains, and as such acquired a

LEFT A broad gauge train crossing a typical Brunel trestle viaduct of the type which were commonplace on his lines in Cornwall, South Devon and South Wales and allowed railways to be built across hilly terrain at affordable cost. The frequent use of such 'cheaper' structures greatly facilitated the expansion of the broad gauge empire.

unique status on the national network. It survives today on the waterfront as a cafe.

In 1862, an Act of Parliament passed for the construction of a broad-gauge branch line from Moretonhampstead to Newton Abbot, the route opening as the Moretonhampstead & South Devon Railway on 26 June 1862. The line was absorbed in 1872 by the South Devon Railway which in turn became part of the GWR empire.

It was not the last broad-gauge line to be built, but by then the writing for the 7ft 0¼in gauge was on the wall.

Did Brunel ever think that, in the face of opposition from the likes of leading authorities like Stephenson, his broad gauge, while superior in so many respects, would ever be adopted as the norm throughout Britain, or did he envisage a super-efficient regional service serving just part of it, with passengers and goods being switched to the smaller trains of other companies wherever the 'break of gauge occurred'?

Had his system 'got in first', and had been adopted by main line railways everywhere, how different would our national transport network be today.

**RIGHT** Firefly class 2-2-2 Load Star and its express train came unstuck at Carmarthen while hauling the 9.15am from Haverfordwest on 8 January 1855.

**FAR RIGHT** Exeter St David's was not only the terminus of the Bristol & Exeter Railway, but the gateway to Brunel's expanding west of England empire. GWR 4-2-2 Emperor stands at Exeter in 1889.

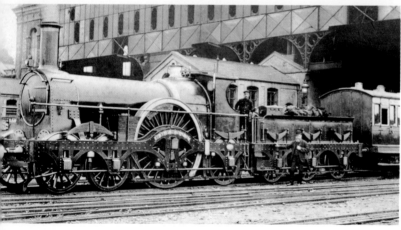

LEFT Torre station, pictured in 1870, was the place where the South Devon Railway's Torquay branch met the Torbay & Dartmouth Railway, also engineered by Isambard Brunel, part of which today operates regular Great Western steam as the Paignton & Dartmouth Steam Railway. The passenger locomotive in the picture is Avonside Engine company 4-4-0 Zebra, which became GWR No 2127. Torre remains an excellent example of a Brunel station, but Isambard surveyed more than just railways at Torbay. He bought 136 acres of land at Watcombe and designed a house in which he wanted to live with his family, surrounded by landscape gardens and an arboretum, but he completed only the foundations before he died. The completed Brunel Manor House is now run by the Woodlands House of Prayer Trust as a Christian holiday and conference centre.

# Chapter 10

# Go Great Western: To New York
## *The first transatlantic liners*

While the new breed of steam-railway magnates was busy carving up Britain, the eyes of Isambard Brunel were already set on a far greater goal.

He wanted to extend his Great Western Railway from London, beyond Bristol – all the way to the United States.

At one stage in his career, Brunel had been touring the country touting for work. Soon, there would come a day when he would become the ultimate workaholic – tackling not one, but several world-beating projects back-to-back.

While he was overseeing the building of the GWR, a project that in itself would have placed him among the greatest engineers of all time; he was busy working on a new and very different project of monumental proportions – the world's first transatlantic liners.

Shipping was the last major area to benefit from the massive strides in transport technology, which had been spawned by the Industrial Revolution, and in the 1830s, still owed more to traditional building techniques than the application of modern science.

Just as railways had been the preserve of horsepower until the Rainhill Trials of 1829, so shipping had been based on developments of sail power, with the industry slow to take up the new steam technology.

What Richard Trevithick was to steam-powered road and rail locomotives, William Symington was to steamboats.

Symington was born in Leadhills, Lanarkshire, in 1764, the son of a mechanic who worked the local lead mines, and like Trevithick, became a pioneer in steam mining technology.

Having worked on perfecting one of James Watt's stationary steam engines, Symington was approached by Patrick Miller, banker and shareholder in Carron Company, Scotland's premier engineering firm, to fit a steam engine inside a pleasure boat for small-scale trials. The aim of this early experiment was to demonstrate that an engine could work on the unstable foundation of a boat, and would not set it on fire.

The engine had already been demonstrated on a model steam carriage, which Symington had built in 1785. The partly successful trial took place on the loch next to Miller's house at Dalswinton, near Dumfries, on 14 October 1788.

Miller was so impressed he ordered a larger engine to undergo tests in a paddleboat on the Forth and Clyde Canal on 2 December 1789 and, after several trials, it reached a speed of nearly 7mph.

Thomas, Lord Dundas, governor of the Forth and Clyde Canal Company, looked into the possibility of using steam tugs along the lines of a prototype trialled by Captain John Schank on the Bridgewater Canal, near Manchester in 1799.

He asked for a Symington engine to be added to a Schank-designed boat, which was successfully given a run-out on the River Carron in June 1801, but was ruled unsuitable for the canal. Symington patented a horizontal engine in 1801, which was more powerful, and won the support of Lord Dundas for a second vessel – to be named Charlotte Dundas, after one of his daughters – to be built.

It was launched in Glasgow on 4 January 1803 and after some later modifications, towed two loaded vessels along the canal, covering 18½ miles in nine-and-a-quarter hours.

Sadly, the canal company turned it down, because of fears it would damage the navigation's banks, and it was forced to live out its life in one of the waterway's passing bays.

Symington, like Trevithick, ended his days fraught with financial difficulties, but nonetheless, his Charlotte Dundas had staked its claim to being the world's first viable steamship.

The launch in 1812 of Henry Bell's Comet on the Clyde – the first steam-operated commercial ferry, was followed two years later by the steamboat Regent, plying its trade between London and Margate. Its designer? Marc Brunel, who again showed he was more than up to speed with cutting-edge technology.

The first cross-channel steamship was the 112-ton Hibernia, which made it from Holyhead to Dublin in seven hours in 1816. The first oceanic crossing by a steamship was made in 1819 by the PS Savannah, built by Francis Fickett, of Corlears Hook, New York; with an engine provided by Stephen Vail of the Speedwell Iron Works, New Jersey.

Originally intended for the sail packet service to Le Havre, it set out from Savannah, Georgia, reaching Liverpool on 20 June, after 29 days 11 hours. However, the engines were sparingly used and for the most part, the ship relied on its sails.

Up to 1835, steamships were still considered suitable only for short runs in comparatively shallow waters, as the early examples did not have the capacity to carry and burn sufficient coal for anything like a transatlantic voyage.

It was considered by leading authorities, including Marc Brunel, that the consumption of coal by a steam engine would increase in proportion to the size of a ship, and if the existing vessels could not manage to cross an ocean, logic dictated that neither could a larger one.

It needed a genius to rewrite the principles of the 'logic' of the day, someone who had already showed himself capable of doing just that.

Isambard realised that this principle was erroneous, as the energy needed to drive a ship, whether by sail or steam, did not depend on the vessel's weight, but on the weight of the water that it had to shift.

**BELOW** The Great Western in the Bristol Channel off Portishead, after leaving the safety of the Avon estuary on her first transatlantic voyage, as seen in a contemporary Joseph Walter oil painting.

**BELOW** The SS Great Britain after being refloated in Sparrow Cove on the Falkland Islands.

He worked out that the key factors were the surface area of the ship, and its shape, and found that contrary to previous belief, the larger the vessel; the more favourable the crucial energy-to-weight equation would be.

At an early meeting of the GWR board, Isambard was said to have suggested extending the railway by adding a steamboat – to be called the Great

Western, after the company – and which would go all the way to New York.

One of the directors, Thomas Guppy, did not join in with the ensuing scorn, and persuaded three other board members, Robert Scot, Robert Bright and Thomas Pycroft to set up a committee to look into the possibility. They were joined by naval captain Christopher Claxton, who Brunel had met while working on the improvements to the city docks, and who was able to gain access to official drawings of Admiralty vessels currently under construction.

A low-key prospectus called for the company to build not one, but two, 1200-ton steamships with 400-horse-power engines. Many local people bought shares in the scheme, including Isambard.

A new prospectus was issued before the first meeting of a new Great Western Steamship Company on 3 March 1836, giving further details of the proposed ships and the estimated cost of £35,000 each. Five of the directors were also board members of the GWR.

Isambard roped in Bristol shipbuilder William Patterson to add his weight and expertise to the project. It was inside Patterson's yard at Wapping Wharf, in the Floating Harbour, that the keel of the first ship was laid in June that year, without pomp or ceremony. At 205ft, it was the longest ever to have been laid.

The ship was clearly so huge that sceptics were again at the fore, doubting whether it could ever be brought out of the dock and down the winding mud of the Avon Gorge to the Bristol Channel, let alone set out to sea.

Lambeth manufacturer Maudslay, Son & Field had vast experience in building marine engines and was selected to supply the ship's engines, which had massive cylinders with a 73½in diameter and a stroke of 7ft, and were to drive twin-paddle wheels 28ft in diameter.

The great day came on 19 July 1837, when more than 50,000 onlookers crowded into Bristol's docks and on to adjacent vessels to watch the ship's launch.

As the ship started moving down the shipway, a deafening cry of 'She moves!' soared to the sky, as Claxton smashed a bottle of madeira over the bowsprit.

Mrs Miles, wife of one of the steamship company's directors, named the ship the Great Western. Afterwards, 300 invited guests joined the directors for dinner in the ship's main cabin.

On 18 August, the Great Western was towed down the Avon estuary by the steam tug Lion, and, accompanied by the steam packet Ben Ledi, using a four-masted schooner rig to travel to London around the south coast of England as a sailing ship.

The London crowds were equally ecstatic when they glimpsed the Great Western for the first time, if only for her sheer size.

In East India Dock at Blackwall, much of the machinery was fitted by Maudslay over an intensive six-month period, and in March 1838, the Great Western was moved to a berth in the River Thames for preliminary trials, during which the ship struck another vessel and days later became briefly stuck on a mud bank opposite Trinity Wharf.

However, four days of engine trials saw the Great Western comfortably manage an average speed of 11 knots.

Isambard had again silenced his critics, including a Dr Dionysius Lardner, who had publicly proclaimed in 1835 that transatlantic steamship travel was all but impossible, discouraging would-be investors from the steamship company.

The British & American Steam Navigation Company's new vessel, the British Queen, would not pip the Great Western to the post as regards making a maiden voyage, and so the firm hired another ship, the 703-ton Sirius, with which it intended to make the first scheduled steamship crossing to the United States. The Sirius set out with 22 passengers in March 1838, while the engines on the Great Western were still being tested.

At last, on 31 March, the Great Western set off for Bristol with Isambard on board to collect the passengers for her maiden voyage. However, around noon, with the ship moving down the Thames, flames and smoke began pouring from the engine room. The boiler lagging had become too hot and caught fire.

The ship's captain, Lieut Hosken, grounded the Great Western on soft mud while the fire was extinguished, but Isambard, descending a ladder to the boiler room, stepped on a burned rung and fell 20ft, badly injuring himself.

But, in the cut-throat world of business, being proved right counts for nothing if others are quicker to take up on your innovations than you are.

North Atlantic shipping companies in both London and Liverpool had watched the coming together of the Great Western with immense interest, and as it entered its final stages of completion, began to convert existing ships in order that they could compete with her.

**RIGHT** One of Bristol's real – and mostly overlooked – architectural treasures is the surviving face of what was built as the Royal Western Hotel, designed by RS Pope and Isambard Brunel and finished in 1839. It was intended to provide a luxury stopover for passengers who had arrived in London via his railway, and were to travel onwards to New York by liner. However, it closed down as early as 1855, and the bulk of the building behind the façade was later demolished to make way for modern offices, which now house a city council department.

The Great Western arrived in Bristol on 2 April, only to find that many of the passengers had cancelled their bookings because of rumours, which had spread about the ship's 'failings'.

With just seven passengers on board, the Great Western set out in pursuit of the Sirius on 7 April. It arrived in New York at noon on 23 April, having made the crossing in just 17 days – only to see the Sirius, which had run aground there the previous night, after exhausting almost all of its coal supply – already moored there.

The Americans were enthralled by the race between the two ships, and so many people wanted to board the Great Western that the captain was forced to issue tickets in order to control numbers. On the return journey, the Great Western reached Britain in just 14 days, as compared to the 18 taken by her rival, and proved that unlike its competitor, it could cross the Atlantic with passengers

and cargo and still have coal to spare.

The Great Western proved to be another world-beater for Isambard, and was an immediate commercial success, making 67 crossings in eight years and silencing her critics for good.

However, she could not fit through the lock gates leading into the Floating Harbour, and accrued high mooring charges by having to be moored in King's Road in the Bristol Channel.

When it left Bristol for New York on 11 February 1843, it would be the last departure of a transatlantic liner from the port for 28 years. In turn, Bristol's importance as a port for Atlantic trade went into decline, and all because the harbour authorities refused to widen the lock gates for new, bigger ships to pass.

Taken out of service at Liverpool in 1846, the Great Western was sold to the Royal Mail Steam Packet Company and used on voyages to the Gulf of Mexico for 10 years, after which she ended her days as a troop ship during the Crimean War, before being scrapped in 1857.

Never one to take a well-deserved rest, in September 1838, Isambard and his committee began planning their second ship.

Initial thoughts by Isambard, Guppy and Claxton turned to a bigger 254ft-long oak ship with even bigger paddle wheels, but they were stopped in their tracks when an iron-hulled paddle steamer, the Rainbow, docked

ABOVE The Floating Harbour with the Avon Gorge and Isambard Brunel's Clifton Suspension Bridge in the background. Two ships he designed and which were destined to change the world left Bristol through here.

in Bristol. Claxton and Paterson sailed in the ship to Antwerp to record her performance.

The first iron-hulled vessel had appeared in 1787, a 70ft-long canal barge, built by John 'Iron Mad' Wilkinson, a partner in the successful project to build the world's first iron bridge over the Severn Gorge, and who, on his death in 1808, was buried in his native Cumberland in an iron coffin.

Medium-sized ocean-going iron-hulled ships were being produced in Britain in the 1820s, and had the advantage of being 30 per cent lighter than their wooden counterparts. The first iron steamship, the Aaron Derby, was built in 1821, but was on nowhere near the scale proposed by Isambard for the company's second ship.

The Brunel committee sat down to work, and between September 1838 and June the following year, six different designs were produced. Eventually chosen was Isambard's 'box-girder' type hull with a two-skinned cellular construction, having six watertight compartments and two longitudinal bulkheads, plus a strong iron deck.

The keel for the new vessel, nick-named the 'Mammoth' was laid on 19

BRUNEL

**FAR LEFT** The SS Great Britain is now the jewel in the crown of the waterfront where it was built, and is a focal point for the Brunel 200 celebrations in 2006.

**LEFT** Memorial picture of Isambard Kingdom Brunel in the Illustrated London News.

Liverpool aboard her.

His report impressed the steamship company to the extent that they ordered all work on the paddle steamers for their second vessel to stop, and booked the Archimedes for six months of tests.

Isambard saw that a fully immersed propeller would be far more efficient than paddle wheels, and in December 1840 insisted that the new ship should be driven exclusively by one.

The decision delivered a fatal blow to ambitious young engineer, Francis Humphrys, who had been chosen by the directors above Maudslay (and against Isambard's advice) to build what would have been the world's biggest marine engine for the ship as originally planned. Told to redesign the paddle engines, which were already at an advanced stage, he resigned and died of a 'brain fever' a few days after his work was halted.

July 1839, again in Patterson's yard.

Isambard was captivated by the sight of the world's first propeller-driven ship, Francis Pettit Smith's Archimedes, when it arrived in the Floating Harbour in May 1840, and Guppy took a trip to

Without an engine for the new ship,

the project was delayed for two years while Brunel and Smith carried out more research into propellers. During this time, they designed an 800-ton experimental sloop, the Rattler, for the Navy. During a tug-of-war contest in April 1845, when attached to the Alecto, a paddle-driven vessel of similar size, the Rattler towed it backwards at a speed of more than two knots. Isambard had backed the winning horse yet again.

With Humphrys gone, Isambard designed the 1600-horsepower engines himself, based on the triangle type patented by his father. The company had leased land next to the Floating Harbour and developed the site into the world's first integrated steamship works, building the engines inside.

The cost of the project soared, ending up at £125,555 – double that of the Great Western, but, buoyed by the success of his GWR, Isambard's project managed to attract sufficient investors.

The ship was launched on 19 July 1843, exactly six years after that of the Great Western.

Prince Albert, arrived from London via the GWR on a special train driven by Daniel Gooch to take his place as guest of honour, after being greeted by the Lord Mayor at Temple Meads station.

Marc and Sophia Brunel watched proudly as the dry dock was flooded to allow their son's giant creation to float.

Mrs Miles was again brought forward to name the ship, but the bottle of champagne missed its target. Prince Albert stepped forward to complete the job and smash a second bottle on the bow, naming the ship the SS Great Britain – a flagship for a country in a world it was beginning to dominate through its empire.

After the ceremony, the SS Great Britain was moved back into the dry dock for fitting out. She was ready in March 1844, but then it was discovered that she was too big to pass through the locks, which linked the Floating Harbour to the Avon estuary.

Isambard was the dock company's consulting engineer, and persuaded its directors to allow modifications to be made to allow the SS Great Britain to pass the Junction Lock into Cumberland Basin, which it did on 26 October 1844, after a delicate and daunting day-long operation.

Trials were undertaken in the Bristol Channel on 12 December and 10 and

20 January before the SS Great Britain made a 40-hour voyage to London on 23 January, averaging 12½ knots, despite bad weather.

She was moored on the Thames for five months; Queen Victoria and Prince Albert were given a guided tour of the ship on 22 April 1845. With a displacement of 3675 tons, compared to 2300 for the Great Western, the SS Great Britain was the biggest ship in the world.

Its first Atlantic crossing was made from Liverpool on 26 July, carrying only 45 passengers and arriving in New York just 15 days later at an average speed of more than nine knots. During her second trip to the USA, the SS Great Britain sustained damage to the propeller and returned to Liverpool under sail power only, but still in only 20 days.

A four-bladed propeller replaced Isambard's experimental six-bladed version, and a third voyage was made to New York on 29 May 1846. On the homeward journey, the SS Great Britain

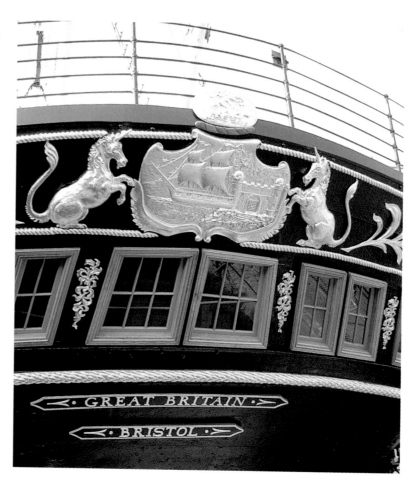

made the crossing in just 13 days, at an average speed of 13 knots.

The ship's fifth trip, however, was an unmitigated disaster. With 180 passengers on board, it ran aground in Dundrum Bay in Ireland, on 22 September, with Captain Hosken, claiming his instruments had been affected by the iron hull and leading him to believe that he was off the coast of the Isle of Man.

There were no fatalities, and while the ship had been holed in two places, its strength prevented it from breaking up.

Claxton built a succession of two breakwaters around the beached ship to protect her, but to no avail, and with the finances of the steamship company also sailing close to the wind, Isambard finally went out to Ireland, to order a protective barrier of 5000 faggots to be piled against the side of the ship, which faced the sea.

After many efforts, the SS Great Britain was finally towed off the beach, by HMS Birkenhead on 27 August 1847.

However, its owners could not afford the £22,000 repairs on top of the £12,670 towing charge, and auctioned off all of her fixtures and fittings before finally selling her to Liverpool shipping firm Bright, Gibbs & Co for a knockdown £18,000.

The Great Western Steamship Company was wound up in February 1852 and the lease on its dockyard sold to Patterson.

New engines were installed for the Great Western's comeback voyage in May 1852, after which the ship spent 24 successful years working the route to Australia. In 1876 she was bought by Antony Gibbs, Sons & Co for use as a transatlantic cargo sailing ship.

After difficulties rounding Cape Horn in April 1886, during which two masts were lost and severe leaks sprung, shelter was sought at Port Stanley in the Falkland Islands.

Estimates for repairs proved too costly, and the ship was sold to the Falkland Islands Company as a store ship for coal and wood.

In 1937, the SS Great Britain was towed out of the harbour and beached at Sparrow Cove, with holes knocked in her stern to ensure that she would never float again.

Thankfully, that was not the end of the story.

The pioneers of transport preservation have made great advances in the post-war decades, not only in the fields of railway and canal heritage and the saving of historic aircraft, but also in shipping.

Interest in saving the SS Great Britain started in the USA and England during the 1950s, and in 1968, a naval architect visited the Falklands to see if it was possible to refloat her.

It was indeed possible, with the aid of a pontoon submerged beneath her hull. With the pontoon pumped out, the ship lifted on top of it.

The SS Great Britain was able to make one last voyage atop the pontoon, making the 7000 miles home, towed behind the salvage tug Varius II. The journey began on 24 April 1970, via Montevideo, and took until 22 June, when they arrived off the Welsh coast, where Bristol tugs were waiting to take the pontoon into the docks at Avonmouth.

The SS Great Britain received a hero's welcome in the port, and soon after, was lifted off the pontoon in the graving dock.

Finally, on 5 July, thousands of spectators again lined the banks of the Avon estuary as the ship, now afloat in its own right, was towed upstream to Bristol's docks. She waited a fortnight for a spring tide high enough to allow

her to be eased into the Great Western dry dock off the Floating Harbour.

The date was 19 July, 127 years to the day that she was launched in 1843.

The meticulous restoration of the SS Great Britain, which is now recognised as having begun a revolution in international shipping, took 35 years to complete, and it is now a major attraction for tourists who come to see her in dry dock on one of the world's greatest waterfronts.

The construction of a 'glass sea' at the waterline of the restored ship acts as a giant airtight chamber protecting its lower hull. Beneath the glass plate, moisture is removed from the air using special dehumidification equipment, preventing further corrosion of the hull. What was once the world's biggest ship is now encased in one of the world's biggest display cases.

The 'glass sea' is covered with a thin layer of water, so the ship appears to be floating. However, visitors can descend beneath the glass to see the ship's hull and its key component, the propeller.

It will now stay moored in the dry dock, as a lasting monument to a man who shrank the world with his vision of transatlantic travel.

# Chapter 11

# How The West Was Finally Won

## *The bridge at Saltash and beyond*

In 814AD, the Saxons under Egbert conquered Cornwall, the last Celtic kingdom in the south-west, although he left the native rules in place. A century later, King Alfred's grandson, Athelstan, made an all-out effort to bring Cornwall under English rule, but it would not be so easily tamed.

The River Tamar remained, for the most part, not only a great physical divide but a psychological and cultural one too. Cornishmen often thought of their homeland as a separate country, referring to Devon as 'England'.

Nine hundred years later, the Tamar remained the last frontier for the great transport pioneers to conquer in order to bring the railway into the Duchy, where it would serve the mineral-rich mining areas and convey their products to markets far and wide.

The word Tamar is far older than English or Cornish. It has its roots in the ancient Sanskrit word for dark, which also presents itself in other British river names such as Tame, Teme, Thame, and Thames.

Just as Isambard had conquered the Thames with bridges everyone who knew better said would never stand up, so he was to accomplish what nobody else had ever believed possible – master the Tamar at its widest point.

Before the mid-19th century, the lowest crossing of the river was at New Bridge at Gunnislake, a local mining

**LEFT** The late great railway artist Terence Cuneo had a mouse as his trademark, and in this magical cartoon of the completion of the Royal Albert Bridge, the rodent became crossed with Isambard Kingdom Brunel. Was it from the same family that gnawed the leather flap on the atmospheric South Devon Railway and forced its early closure, I wonder?

town. It was by then not so new, having been built in 1520 to carry the road from Callington to Tavistock.

If you wanted to cross below this point, such as from Plymouth to Torpoint or Saltash, boat was the only way. Until Isambard Brunel appeared, with his determination to turn one of his greatest dreams into reality – to run a railway from Paddington to Penzance.

The Cornwall Railway was promoted in late 1844, just after Brunel had completed the Bristol & Exeter Railway. Captain William Moorsom, who had been involved with the Bristol & Gloucester Railway eight years previously, was asked by local businessmen in 1843 to survey a line and draw up plans for a 66-mile line from the South Devon Railway at Plymouth to the naval port of Falmouth.

He talked of a 'floating bridge' or train ferry to cross the Hamoaze, the name given to the estuary of the tidal Tamar opposite Devonport, and had at first considered to work the Cornish line by atmospheric propulsion.

After the first scheme was thrown out by the House of Lords, Isambard replaced Moorsom and was appointed engineer for the project, and carried

out a new survey, this time calling for a high-level bridge across the Tamar.

This vastly improved plan was passed by Parliament on 3 August 1846, and as expected, Isambard opted again for broad gauge.

An alternative 1845 proposal for a Central Cornwall Railway, taking the time-honoured coach road through the middle of the county, and backed by the GWR's great rival-to-be, the London & South Western Railway, failed to win approval.

However, while drawing up that scheme, the LSWR had bought out Cornwall's first public railway, the Bodmin & Wadebridge, in the vain hope of using it as part of the route. The action left the LSWR with a 'white elephant' to which it would not connect for 40 years, but it dashed Cornwall Railway's hopes of a broad-gauge branch to the port of Padstow.

Work on the Cornwall Railway began at Truro in 1847, but little work was done for several years because money kept running out. This was the time when the first great wave of Railway Mania was beginning to falter and backers for schemes were becoming scarce.

Meanwhile, further west in the Duchy,

**LEFT** All alone –
before the coming of
the modern suspension
bridge, Brunel's rail
crossing of the Tamar
as seen in the early
20th century.

the standard-gauge Hayle Railway opened in 1837, running from Hayle Foundry to Pool and Portreath, and extending to Redruth the following year. Its primary aim was to connect the Redruth-Camborne mining areas to the coast, and steam locomotives were used from the start over most of its system.

On 3 August 1846, the West Cornwall Railway received authorisation and took over the Hayle Railway, intending eventually, to convert it to broad gauge, extend it to Penzance in one direction and Truro in the other, thereby meeting up with the future Cornwall Railway. Isambard was brought in as engineer on the West Cornwall too, and became chairman of its board from 1847-8.

Under Isambard's jurisdiction, the West Cornwall was completed between Penzance and a temporary Truro terminus in 1851, opening on 11 March 1852.

While mineral traffic on the line was of paramount importance, the West Cornwall opened up the prospect of easier travel to London for those living at the far end of the county for the first time. You could travel from Penzance or

Truro to Hayle, take the paddle steamer packet service on to Bristol and travel onwards by the GWR.

Isambard's Cornwall Railway route involved 34 viaducts over the 53 miles between Plymouth and Truro, built in timber, just like several that had been on the later sections of the South Devon Railway, including the 670ft-long Ivybridge Viaduct, and also the 1760ft Landore Viaduct in South Wales.

Nine more were to follow on the West Cornwall, as a total of eight river estuaries and 30 valleys were crossed.

His distinctive trestle structures – known as fan viaducts because of the shape of the supports – involved timber constructions of masonry pillars, and were a cost-effective way of crossing the steep Cornish terrain.

These were far longer and more complex than his first timber bridge, a five-span affair, which carried a public road across Sonning cutting.

Although they were all were replaced from the late 19th century onwards with more expensive and longer-lasting stone alternatives, the old columns can still be seen standing alongside the new crossings at places like Moorswater.

Mindful of criticism that wood, mainly Baltic pine, could rot away, the viaducts were designed by Brunel in such a way that any offending timbers could be unbolted and replaced without having to close the line. Many of them lasted for 60 years, and it was only after the price of timber became too high after the outbreak of WWI that there was a mass movement to replace them with masonry.

The last to survive in Cornwall was College Wood Viaduct on the Falmouth branch, which stayed in situ until 1934.

In a bid to revive the stalled project, following years in the financial doldrums, Isambard announced in 1851 that he had found contractors to build the Cornwall Railway for £800,000, albeit single rather than double track, but the offer was not taken up. Hopes rose again when contracts for the key Plymouth-Saltash section were placed the following year.

The GWR, Bristol & Exeter and South Devon Railway took on a partial lease of the project from 1855, and continued to bail it out as construction proceeded in piecemeal fashion. It was left to Isambard to tackle the biggest hurdle of them all – the Tamar, which at Saltash is 1100ft wide and 70ft deep.

At first he suggested building a timber bridge with one main span of 255ft and

six further spans of 105ft each, but the Navy insisted that any crossing must allow headroom of 100ft to clear the masts of tall ships.

He then suggested a single-span bridge to clear the estuary in one fell swoop, but the estimated £500,000 cost was way beyond the reaches of the Cornwall Railway. Isambard then came up with a truly stunning and radical design, which more than made up for his disastrous fling with atmospheric propulsion, a mode by now long deleted from the Cornwall Railway scheme.

His Tamar crossing featured two arched tubular girders, fastened to four cast-iron columns in the middle of the river, supporting by suspension a pair of 450ft spans, which would carry a single-track railway from one side of the river to another – a double-track version had been slimmed down, again to save money.

After test borings beneath the mud of the riverbed, a huge wrought-iron cylinder was sunk in the middle of the estuary, after a highly complex and elaborate operation.

Inside, workmen toiled away in hellish conditions at the bed of the river, digging down to the rock strata so that a solid granite column could be fixed in it. The column supports the cast-iron pillars supporting the great tubular arches.

Isambard drew much from his design for the Usk Bridge at Chepstow, and his use of tubular steel harked back to the far humbler swing bridge at Bristol's Floating Harbour.

The tubular girders were assembled on the east bank and weighed 1060 tons when finished. They were floated across the river into position on pontoons, after a special dock was cut in the Devon bank, and jacked up with hydraulic presses to the required height; this truly spectacular

**LEFT** This third section of a Cornwall Railway broad-gauge coach from the mid-19th century ended up being used as a track ganger's hut in Grampound Road, from where it was retrieved by National Railway Museum staff in 1977 and restored for display at its headquarters in York.

operation began on 1 September 1857.

Attached to each tube were the suspension chains, linked to each other by 11 uprights. Diagonal bracing was added to provide extra rigidity.

Isambard had gained vast experience in lifting suspension bridges when he assisted Robert Stephenson in the construction of the Conway and Britannia bridges in North Wales.

The great bridge, which has an overall length of 730 yards, took seven years to build and cost £225,000. Despite the colossal expense by the day's standards, the directors of the Cornwall Railway heaped praise on him, knowing that it would outlive their lifetimes and many

more, acknowledging that it was nonetheless a truly economic solution.

After his death, the inscription, I K BRUNEL ENGINEER 1859, was ordered to be displayed above the entry arches in perpetuity. Everyone who travelled to Cornwall and passed through the unique structure would immediately be told the name of its designer.

By the time the bridge was finished, the remainder of the Plymouth-Truro line had been completed, all ready for the first trains.

The structure was named the Royal Albert Bridge, as it was the Prince Consort who opened it officially on 2 May 1859.

Both banks of the river were packed with onlookers, while others crowded on hills and rooftops overlooking the river, desperate for a glimpse of the proceedings. A flotilla of steamers and small boats plied their way up the Hamoaze for a grandstand view. The last county in Britain without a link to the national rail network was now connected.

VIPs from Cornwall, including the mayors of Truro and Penzance, arrived by train and were presented to the prince. The following day, a grand civic banquet was held in the Town Hall at Truro to serve guests who had arrived on a special train, which left Plymouth at 10.30am and arrived shortly before 1pm.

It was said that everyone living in the towns and villages along the route had turned out to cheer and wave the train on as it passed.

On 4 May, the Cornwall Railway was opened to the public. At last the county, which had produced Richard Trevithick,

LEFT A colour postcard of Brunel's viaduct in Truro, highlighting the typical fan-like construction of the supports. Although replaced in 1902, five of the piers survive in Victoria Gardens. These 'cheap' yet sturdy viaducts enabled the Plymouth to Penzance lines to be built.

The final part of the original Cornwall Railway route, from Truro to Falmouth, had to wait another four years before it was opened. Work had begun in 1850, but stopped when the contractor failed. Renewed calls for its completion were made loudly in 1861 when new docks at Falmouth were completed, and it finally opened on 24 August 1863.

By then, however, Falmouth had declined in importance in transport terms, with the Royal Mail Packet Service fleet having been transferred from here to Southampton, after more than 150 years. The result was that the line to Truro would remain a branch line, not the intended main line, which now ran on to Penzance.

inventor of the first railway locomotive, was connected to the national network, and thereby to London. The world had suddenly grown much smaller, and the Tamar was, for the first time in history, no more a barrier.

One important person was sadly absent from the opening celebrations. Isambard Brunel.

In deteriorating health, he was too ill to attend, but did manage to ride across the bridge a few days later, lying couch mounted, on a truck pulled by a Gooch engine.

In 1864, the Cornwall Railway exercised its right to demand that the West Cornwall, which was still standard gauge, laid a broad-gauge rail to accommodate through trains. It could not afford it, and so it was leased to the consortium of the GWR, Bristol & Exeter and South

Devon Railway, which immediately laid the third rail.

At last, on 1 March 1867, a through service between Paddington and Penzance was begun, with locomotives supplied by the South Devon Railway. At last, the great dream of those who had launched the GWR more than a third of a century before had been realised, and the future tourist trade of the West Country was assured.

Furthermore two subsequent offshoots of the West Cornwall deserve special mention.

A branch nearly five miles long from St Erth on the mainline, to St Ives was authorised in 1876 and opened on 1 June 1877. It was the last new Brunel broadgauge line to be built, and became the property of the GWR the following year.

The short standard-gauge Hayle Wharf branch had a third rail added when it was extended along the quaysides, and opened for goods traffic only on 3 October 1877.

Cornwall is famous for its sunsets, and here was the twilight of Isambard's 7ft 0¼in gauge empire, which had stretched from London, north to Wolverhampton and westwards to Milford Haven and now Penzance.

FAR LEFT A Class 37 diesel on the Looe branch in the 1980s at Moorswater. Note the surviving stumps of Brunel's Cornwall Railway wooden trestle viaduct rear in front of the later replacement.

LEFT The wooden viaduct on the South Devon Railway main line at Ivybridge was typical of the type which made the building of Brunel's Cornwall Railway economically possible.

The Royal Albert Bridge has been strengthened several times since it was built, and the station at Saltash at the western end still retains its original 1859 building.

In the Macmillan years when we 'never had it so good,' the car became king as more and more people could afford to buy one, and as a result many West Country branch lines began to close, even before Dr Richard Beeching wielded his axe in 1963.

The following year, a second Tamar crossing was opened alongside Brunel's, a modern suspension bridge taking the A38 from Plymouth to Saltash, replacing the car ferry that ran below.